CROCODILES & ALLIGATORS
OF THE
WORLD

CROCODILES & ALLIGATORS
OF THE
WORLD

David Alderton

Photography by
Bruce Tanner

BLANDFORD

Paperback edition first published in the UK 1992
by Blandford, a Cassell imprint

Cassell plc,
Wellington House
125 Strand
London
WC2R OBB

Reprinted 1998

Previously published in hardback by Blandford in 1991

Distributed in the United States by
Sterling Publishing Co., Inc.,
387 Park Avenue South, New York, NY 10016–8810

A Cataloguing-in-Publication Data entry for this title is available
from the British Library

ISBN 0–7137–2382–3

Typeset in the UK by August Filmsetting, Haydock, St Helens

Printed and bound by Colorcraft Ltd, Hong Kong

Contents

Acknowledgements

All photographs were taken by Bruce Tanner, except Plates 2, 9, 33, 41, 47, 48, 49, 60, 71 and 72, which were taken by the author.

The line illustrations were drawn by Mike Alderton.

Grateful thanks are due to the many people who assisted in the preparation of this book, with a particular debt being due to the following:

Liz Carveth; John Cheetham, Beaver Water World, Tatsfield, Kent; Department of Conservation, Tallahassee, Florida; Everglades Gator Farm, Hamstead, Florida; Dr Jurgen Lange, Zoologischer Garten, Berlin; Thomas Condie and Bill Zeigler at Miami Metrozoo, Florida; George Oxendale, HM Customs and Excise, London; Col Fuller and staff of the Conservation Commission of the Northern Territory, Australia.

In addition, Rita Hemsley again managed to read my handwriting to produce the typescript, and Stuart Booth provided invaluable editorial support. Thanks are also due to Helen Sell and my wife, Jacqueline, for preparing the index.

Preface

It is surprising how much our view of the natural world is conditioned in childhood. Some creatures, such as the giant panda or koala, are instinctively appealing. Others, like snakes or crocodiles, often evoke strong feelings of fear. People will give readily to save cuddly endangered species. If 77 per cent of a group of these species were on the verge of extinction, there would be grave concern and immediate finance would be forthcoming for conservation projects. The crocodilians of the world lack this advantage. Perceived for far too long as dangerous killers, their cause engenders little public sympathy.

Yet crocodilians rank amongst the oldest surviving vertebrate groups, dating directly from the age of the dinosaurs. They practise a degree of parental care and social communication unrivalled in the lower vertebrates. At the very most, only six out of the 22 surviving species represent any danger to people.

Most crocodilians have been brought to their imperilled state during the present century, often hunted to the very verge of extinction for their skins. Yet now, with their habitats under threat in many cases, this demand for their skins could prove to be their salvation. Ranching and farming of crocodilians ensure a supply of hides and also secure surroundings where hatchlings can be reared free from many of the hazards which decimate their numbers in the wild.

Ranching can rapidly boost the populations of endangered species of crocodilians, although it may be a number of years before they can themselves begin to breed. But it gives a greater measure of security and one of the greatest benefits of ranching is that the local people are encouraged to see crocodilians as a sustainable resource, rather than dangerous vermin to be wiped out for their hides. Whether habitats will remain in the long term is a different matter, but governments collectively are beginning to show greater resolve and awareness of the need to protect wildlife habitats throughout the world. The future for the maligned crocodilian is not entirely without hope, especially since it is clear that, under suitable conditions, programmes of reintroduction into the wild do work.

David Alderton
Brighton
England

Chapter 1
History, Legend and Literature

Inevitably, because of the predatory nature of crocodilians, coupled with their large size in many cases, these reptiles have assumed a prominent position in the folklore of many cultures. In ancient Egypt, they were deified, in the form of a crocodile-headed god called Sebek. Worship was centred on the temple dedicated to Sebek at Ombos, and this cult dated back to at least 1800 B.C.

ANCIENT EGYPTIAN ATTITUDES TO CROCODILES

In the province of Fayyum, there was a similar shrine to Sebek at Shedet, which housed a Nile crocodile (*Crocodylus niloticus*) thought to be the incarnation of the god on earth. This particular beast was decorated with gold ornaments, while nearby, other crocodiles, assumed to be relatives of Sebek, were treated with similar respect.

The entire crocodilian dynasty was given a special burial area, located in the south of the province, at Tebtunis. All these crocodiles, and even their eggs, were carefully preserved by embalming. The mummies were then covered in papyrus and wrapped in special preservative bandages before being placed in coffins.

The Egyptians actively encouraged the presence of crocodiles in their canals, possibly to deter illicit incursions into their territory. Certainly the crocodiles appear to have flourished under such protection. Herodotus, the Greek historian, visited the area during the 5th century B.C., and recorded how priests still decorated the tame crocodiles which lived in Lake Mairis with gold ornaments.

Strabo (63 B.C.–A.D. 20) noted how Shedet, by then known as Crocodilopolis, had become famous throughout the classical world for its crocodiles, which were fed literally by hand. As one priest held the reptile's jaws apart, another would place a selection of meat, cakes and bread within, pouring in a milk and honey drink for good measure! This scenario appears to have been repeated each time a traveller brought an offering.

But elsewhere in Egypt, a cult which was essentially hostile towards crocodilians also emerged. Tomb carvings, dating back to the period about 2500 B.C., portray Sebek swimming beneath the boats carrying the ruling pharaohs to the underworld. A crocodile's tail symbolized darkness in hieroglyphic language and Sebek, as a supporter of the night, was blamed for solar eclipses.

In upper Egypt, crocodiles were ruthlessly hunted because they represented the earthly guise of the ruler Set, who had committed fratricide by slaying his brother Osiris. Prior to this, their father Gib had divided Egypt between them, but Set was not satisfied with ruling over half a kingdom.

HEALING POWERS OF CROCODILIANS

As a result of their links with darkness, crocodiles were also held responsible for causing blindness. Certainly in some areas, river blindness resulting from an infection by the parasitic roundworm, *Onchocerca*, was a major problem. In an attempt to offer a cure, the *Ebers Papyrus* gives 92 different prescriptions, many of which rely upon crocodile fat and dung, plus a liberal dose of incantation. The physician would state 'The crocodile is now weak and powerless' as the medication was administered.

The use of crocodile potions apparently grew in popularity. Pliny, in his famous and monumental work *Naturalis Historia*, which appeared in 37 volumes during the first century A.D., held that most ailments could benefit from treatment with crocodilian medication. The meat of crocodiles was thought to assist children afflicted with whooping cough, while burnt crocodile skin combined with vinegar was believed to have anaesthetic properties. The dung of crocodiles, applied in a lint tampon, was even a fashionable contraceptive for women at this time.

The impact of Pliny's advice lasted for centuries and, interestingly, spread in due course to the New World. Here, during the 1880s, those afflicted with a tuberculoid cough were dispensed alligator oil, to act as an emollient, and advised to consume large quantities of the meat of these reptiles, which were then plentiful. There is no evidence to show that these treatments had any beneficial effect.

CROCODILE FOLKLORE IN AFRICA

Crocodile worship has continued in Africa down the intervening centuries. Many potions, for example those produced by the Thonga tribe of southern Zululand, contain crocodile fat. These are said to guard against lightning as well as various ailments. Protection against crocodile attack is also conferred on tribespeople who acquire a tooth or claw and wear it around the neck, especially if the charm in question originates from a known man-eating crocodile.

In Benin (formerly Dahomey) crocodiles, thought to contain malig-

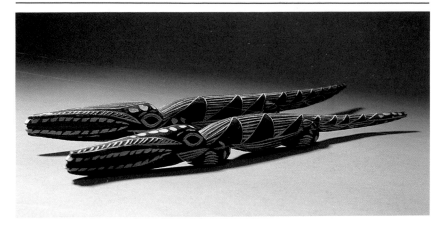

Plate 1   Carvings and other representations of crocodilians are consistently found in cultures in many parts of the world where these reptiles occur. Interestingly, common threads of folklore, such as the supposed mystical power of their teeth, pervaded different continents long before there was any obvious contact between the tribes concerned.

nant spirits which endangered travellers, were kept in ponds near the royal palace. Here the reptiles could be placated regularly by priests, who made offerings to them.

The belief, in Africa, that crocodiles caused blindness was another lingering relic of the Egyptian cult, which was noted during the last century by the explorer David Livingstone. He observed how members of the Crocodile clan, or *Ba-kuena*, who lived in South Africa, tried to avoid any contact with a crocodile, as this was thought to induce a swelling of the eyes. Any tribesperson lucky enough to survive a crocodile attack would still be rejected from the tribe, because it was believed that he or she had come into direct contact with sin.

Yet the *Ba-kuena* viewed the crocodile as their traditional ancestor, and identified their cattle with its image, which they cut into their ears. More gruesome appeasement of crocodile gods persisted even later, into the present century. A British missionary in Africa, the Revd J. Roscoe, described a cult of this type he encountered close to the island of Danba, in Lake Victoria, Uganda.

The priest in charge mimicked the movements of the sacred crocodile when giving pronouncements and human sacrifices were regularly carried out to appease this deity. Prisoners belonging to other tribes had their arms and legs broken and were staked out on the shore of the lake, to be consumed by the crocodiles there. It was believed that this allowed fishermen and others from the tribe to cross the lake in safety.

The judgemental role of the crocodile has also played a part in some African cultures. On the White Nile at Malakal, the Shilluk tribe

11

allowed men accused of adultery to swim the river. If they were attacked by a crocodile, this was taken to be a sign of guilt, and they were left to their fate.

A trial of this nature, sometimes known as *Tangem-Boay*, was often practised by the people of Madagascar. A prisoner was thrown into the water, after the judge had invoked the crocodiles to pass judgement. If the suspect swam safely to the opposite bank and back again, he was considered to be innocent. His accusers then had to provide him with two cattle in return for his ordeal, as well as supplying one each to the judge and the king of the tribe.

Also in Madagascar, as elsewhere, crocodile teeth were thought to act as lucky talismans. In some areas, there is a belief that crocodiles provide an earthly resting place for the spirits of tribal chiefs and so the water is kept clean for them. It was only permitted to hunt and kill a crocodile if it was known to have killed a member of the tribe. Otherwise the crocodiles themselves would seek revenge and seize an innocent villager.

Lake Komakoma had a particular spiritual status, because it was here that the body organs of dead kings were fed to the crocodiles by the Sakalava people. The crocodiles were believed to be the ancestors of the tribespeople and so could not be hunted. The only exception was if a person was killed by one of the crocodiles. Then, using a baited hook to ensnare one of the reptiles, the villagers would kill it with special poles, finally burying its body amidst great mourning.

At Lac Sacre in Madagascar, it became a custom to attract the crocodiles to the shore of the lake, by making a noise, if a member of the village fell ill. Here they were fed on fresh meat, and begged to ask the help of the god Zanahary in assisting the recovery of the sick person.

One stage further from this practice is the appearance of witches in the guise of crocodiles. In Zaïre (formerly the Belgian Congo), there was always an attempt made to find the person involved when a crocodile killed someone. The punishment for this crime in the vicinity of Lake Nyasa was to be fed to the crocodiles.

CROCODILIAN MYTHS IN INDO-PACIFIC CULTURES

The idea that human spirits could dwell in crocodiles was not confined exclusively to Africa. For example, at the mouth of the Cagayan River, on the Philippine island of Luzon, there was a widespread belief that a large crocodile which lived there about the turn of the century actually contained the soul of a dead chief.

Eroticism involving crocodiles has long been a feature of the folklore of many Indonesian islands. Women were traditionally believed to copulate with these reptiles, giving birth to both a child and a crocodile as a consequence. The young crocodile was carefully placed in the water and allowed its freedom, while the family cared for it by leaving food close to the river. As the children grew up, so the responsibility for this task shifted to them. The crocodile would then protect the family from evil, while, on certain feast days, all the villagers would take to the water, calling the crocodiles to them. They would then throw them special foods.

The Haura tribe of Papua even believe they are descended from a crocodile ancestor. But this idea of a human-crocodilian union has assumed more sinister overtones on some islands, such as Timor. Here, each year, the Rajah of Kupang used to insist on sacrificing a virgin girl who was related to him. The poor girl, garlanded with flowers and perfume, was taken to a special cave and chained to a rock. It was believed that, when the crocodile seized her, he was carrying the girl away to become his bride. This would ensure the continuation of the dynasty, which again was supposed to have originated from crocodiles in the past.

Sacrifices of this type were surprisingly widespread. On the Indonesian island of Buru, where crocodiles were proving a problem for villagers, it was decreed that a girl had to be given to a crocodile which had become infatuated with her. Again, the unfortunate girl, dressed in bridal wear, was given up to the crocodiles.

This tradition seems to have permeated quite widely through various Asiatic cultures. Similar rituals were observed elsewhere, in Korea for example, and their origins may be traced back to the days of ancient Egypt. Here it became commonplace to sacrifice virgins when canals were being dug, as a means of appeasing the crocodiles. It was also thought to ensure a continuing supply of water for the crops in the surrounding fields.

The practice continued up to A.D. 642, until the invasion by Amr Ibn-al-As, who declared it illegal. He insisted that replicas of the girls, made of clay or wood, were used instead and this tradition was then maintained for centuries.

Interestingly, as in Africa, crocodile teeth have assumed a particular significance in some Asiatic cultures. They are used by witch-doctors of the Kodal tribe, who live in the Torres Strait between New Guinea and Australia, as a death charm. A hollow tooth is stuffed with herbs, before being painted red and covered in fat from a dead person. Then the sorcerer finds a sapling to form a bow and fires the tooth, imploring it to strike the heart of the victim, as the ritual is concluded.

13

Similarly, crocodile teeth are also seen as a potent torch, able to start a fire in an enemy's house. In turn, the Kodal tribe pay due homage to the power of the crocodile by tattooing their bodies with its image. The scutes of the reptile are fashioned into badges, to be worn by tribal members.

Another African belief about crocodiles, which has appeared in Asia as well, is that human souls may transfer into the body of these reptiles. The reason for this belief may stem from the potential lifespan of crocodilians, which often exceeds that of human beings.

Some Papuan tribes are convinced that people eaten by crocodiles can be seen in the animal's eyes after dark. The eyes of crocodiles become conspicuous at night, when a light is shone over the water, and this may explain how such an unusual belief could have arisen. Should the spirit start to plague the villagers, they will resort to luring the crocodile away up a nearby river. Then, abandoning their canoe, they will return to their village overland. The spirit will be unable to follow them and so the problem will be resolved.

Crocodile imagery once played a central part in puberty rites on the group of Indonesian islands known as the southern Moluccas. Having been passed through the jaws of a replica crocodile, the youths would be taken away from their grieving mothers. They then lived with the village priests who taught them their tribal secrets for several days. When they returned there was great rejoicing in the village that the crocodile had allowed the youths to continue their lives.

Tales about crocodiles are spread widely through the southern Pacific, even to areas such as New Zealand where these reptiles have never been found. Through the tales of countless generations, the image of the crocodile would appear to have become converted into a savage water-dragon. Known as *taniwha*, it is believed to live in underground lairs, seizing unsuspecting children in particular, should they venture away from their village after dark.

The link between crocodilians and the dragons of popular folklore is evident in many societies of Polynesia. On Hawaii, there was thought to be a deity called Kihawahine, who resembled a huge lizard and inhabited a pond close to the royal family, which she protected. A similar god, called Moko, was worshipped on the Cook Islands and, clearly, the description of a giant aquatic lizard-like creature could only be based on a crocodile.

The dragons of China and Japan are also likely to be the result of images based, at least in part, on crocodilians. Certainly the origins of the dragon are reptilian, as archaeological evidence dating back up to 6000 years has revealed. Here crocodilians, as well as lizards, featured in the culture of individual communities. Gradually, it appears that

Plate 2   Crocodiles have featured prominently in the art of the Australian Aborigines, as well as in stories handed down from generation to generation. The oldest known example of Aboriginal rock art depicting a crocodile dates back 30,000 years.

Plate 3   It was widely believed, at least in Europe, that all crocodilians were dangerously aggressive towards people. In reality, however, the majority, especially the narrow-snouted species, rarely inflict injury and prefer to avoid a close encounter.

these totems were fused and embellished, yielding the concept of the dragon. Even today, there is no standardized depiction of the dragon, and clear regional differences are still apparent.

One such dragon is reputed to have provided the inspiration for a written form of Chinese, in about 2800 B.C. Its description and lifestyle are again rather indicative of a crocodile. This particular dragon had a scaly body, with spines running along its back and prominent claws on its legs. In addition, however, it had two horns and whiskers on its flat head.

This dragon was encountered by the sage Fu Hsi as it emerged on to land from the Yangtze River (Jinsha Jiang). He observed the letters on its back and noted them down. They were used for centuries afterwards, as mystic symbols.

The concept of dragons appears to have spread directly from China to Japan. Here, in 1690, a German explorer called Engelbert Kaemfer recalled his encounter with what he believed to be a living dragon. From his description, however, it seems that almost certainly the creature in question was actually a crocodilian. It was kept here in a shrine.

Further south, in Australia, crocodiles have played a significant part in Aboriginal folklore. Here yet again, it was a common belief that the souls of people migrated into these reptiles after their death. Almost certainly, this concept originated further north and was brought to Australia by the ancestors of the Aborigines.

Many examples of rock art on this continent feature representations of crocodiles. One example, at Panaramittee in the state of South Australia, is believed to be 30,000 years old. Again, a recurring theme is the birth of people from crocodiles, which reflects perhaps a realization of the antiquity of the crocodilian lineage, coupled with primitive attempts to explain our own evolutionary history.

Various Aboriginal bark paintings also depict crocodiles, sometimes killing people, or sometimes catching fish. These reflect a clear understanding of the living crocodilian, rather than the mystical representations of these reptiles which tend to be more widespread. The dangers which they could pose for people were graphically portrayed much later in the Victorian painting entitled *Killing an Alligator on the Horseshoe Flats*. It showed the explorer Thomas Baines battling with a large shark-toothed crocodilian which was lunging towards him, while a friend rushed to assist him.

Indeed, one of the reasons that crocodilians achieved such a notorious reputation, certainly in the more primitive cultures, would have been the difficulty in slaying such beasts with simple weapons. The relative speed and agility of the dangerous crocodilians in a close encounter makes them extremely formidable adversaries even today.

16

PEOPLE AND CROCODILIANS IN THE NEW WORLD

Crocodilians played a central part in the culture of many of the early South American tribes. The Olmec tribe, found in eastern Mexico, had a religious cult which included a crocodilian deity. As their influence in the region spread, so did this symbol. Nevertheless, it appears that the Olmec also hunted crocodilians extensively and may actually have exterminated them in some areas. As today, crocodile leather and meat could be traded, with other parts of the body, such as the teeth, perhaps having a religious value. Here crocodilians were thought to be harbingers of good harvests.

This tradition persisted long after the decline of the Olmec, with crocodilian imagery being represented in South American cultures right through to the discovery of the New World by Columbus and the subsequent Spanish invasion. The Mayan civilization portrayed crocodilians alongside their crops and also in aquatic scenes, with waterlilies and fish. Their god, Ah Puch, a symbol of death, was drawn in the shape of a crocodile.

Subsequently, the Aztecs maintained the crocodilian images of their Teotihuacan ancestors, symbolizing agricultural fertility in the form of Cipactli, a crocodilian deity and also in a related form called Tlaloc, who was considered responsible for bringing the rains.

Early European explorers soon fuelled crocodilian myths back in their homelands with tales about these fearsome beasts which they had encountered on their travels. Again, there are clear links with mythical dragons in many of these stories. For example, William Bartram, who travelled in the south east of what is now the USA during the later part of the eighteenth century, described these reptiles as bellowing clouds of smoke from their nostrils and roaring loudly.

Other writers followed in a similar vein, reinforcing this imagery, and even compounding it in some cases. The widespread belief developed that alligators used their tails to sweep likely prey off river-banks into the water. Their teeth were also reputed to be as big as tusks of ivory, emphasizing the supposedly sinister nature of these reptiles.

An anthropologist called William Holmes, who lived alongside the Chiriqui tribe for a period during the last century, noted how these Panamanian Indians had adopted crocodilians in their culture. He was able to trace the conversion of the crocodile image of their ancestors into an almost mythical dragon-like creature which appeared on the contemporary pottery of the tribe.

In South America, the Montana people of Peru have a long-standing tradition that they will be protected from poisoning by wearing a crocodile tooth. Several tribes in the Pomeroon River basin in Guyana believe that the ancestry of woman traces back to a

Plate 4   The native Indians in North America have lived alongside and hunted the American alligator (*Alligator mississippiensis*) since they first settled in the southern part of the continent. Today, rather than hunting alligators, they use them in displays for tourists.

Plate 5   For many people, this will be as close as they want to venture to any crocodilian, but it will doubtless make a good holiday tale when they get home, because of the fear which these reptiles inspire.

Plate 6   Travellers' tales often embellished the image of the crocodilian, building it up to a terrifying, almost mystical, beast. Almost certainly, such stories formed the basis for the legends of dragons, which feature in many cultures. In the eighteenth century, for example, alligators were said to bellow clouds of smoke from their nostrils.

Plate 7   Right from childhood, the image of the crocodile is that of a villain. Here, in a popular 'Punch and Judy' show, Mr Punch wrestles for his sausages with the evil crocodile. Such puppet shows have been performed in Europe and elsewhere since at least the 1600s.

crocodilian. Here the story is told of how an alligator tricked the Sun and this ultimately gave rise to the Carob tribe of Indians.

Being a keen fisherman, the Sun was upset when fish kept disappearing from his ponds at night. So he appointed the alligator to guard the fish, unaware that the reptile was actually the thief. Finally, though, the Sun caught him and slashed his body, forming scales.

In return for his life, the alligator promised to give the Sun his daughter for a wife. This offer was accepted by the Sun and so the alligator, who had no children, was forced to carve a woman from a tree. Since she lacked the anatomical capability to bear him sons, the Sun then rejected the woman and so the alligator asked the woodpecker to complete his endeavours. A snake then emerged from between the woman's thighs, after which the Sun gratefully accepted her, and she bore him twin sons.

Similar stories were apparently told in the Caribbean, with one from Haiti being recorded by Ferdinand Columbus, son of the famous explorer, who visited the island with his father during 1497. Even today in Guyana, teeth as well as scales of crocodilians are thought to be endowed with mystical powers. But why such similar stories have arisen about crocodilians throughout the world, amongst isolated tribes and before the days of European influence, is a mystery.

CROCODILIANS IN LITERATURE

One of the most lasting images about crocodilians that has become established in literature is the concept of a crocodile's tears. These are symbolic of insincerity, with the origins of this myth dating back at least to the mid-sixteenth century. The idea appears to have stemmed from the observations of the infamous sea captain, John Hawkins, who sailed through Caribbean waters regularly. He recorded that the crocodiles used to cry in order to attract prey, ensuring that the report had a strong anthropomorphic appeal.

This belief was then encapsulated into Spenser's famous work *The Faerie Queene*, which was published in 1590. Later writers continued the theme, which achieved widespread popular notoriety, first in the anonymous Victorian nursery rhyme entitled *Natural History*. This asks rhetorically 'What are young men made of?' with the answer being 'Sighs and leers, and crocodile tears'.

Interestingly, the abbreviated form of this rhyme, which substitutes 'little boys' for 'young men' and has become popular during this century, loses the original meaning. The full rhyme extends to four verses. It wryly reflects the change in personality from the mucky innocence of boys to the more sophisticated, but less honest, adolescent.

The image of the crocodile has suffered further at the hands of writers during this century. J.M. Barrie's story of *Peter Pan*, which was originally written as a stage play in 1904, incorporates the evil menace of the crocodile, and has since appeared in many versions, becoming one of the best-known pieces of children's literature.

Contemporary novels, such as Shelley Katz's *Alligator*, often feature savage crocodilians, reinforcing the false beliefs that all such reptiles are dangerous to people and grow to a giant size. There is little public sentiment to be found to assist the conservation of crocodilians as a result; whereas mammals, such as the elephant or giant panda, immediately engender support.

The growth of the film and video industries has done little to assist the cause of the crocodilian in the public's eyes. Some of the most popular releases of recent years have cast crocodilians as menacing killers. These have included various James Bond movies, as well as Paul Hogan's *Crocodile Dundee* films. Rarely are crocodilians portrayed as being one of the oldest vertebrate lifeforms on the planet, with 17 of the remaining 22 species being classed as in grave danger of extinction, making them possibly the last of their line. Thus, it is important that we now consider their current situation and their interaction with our own modern world.

Chapter 2

Crocodilians and Humans Today

It is impossible to estimate the numbers of people who fall victim to crocodile attacks each year. Indeed, in some cases, there is simply no obvious trace left of the person, and their disappearance may remain a mystery. People who live alongside crocodilians, using the lakes and rivers for everyday activities such as washing, often turn to various charms and incantations for protection. But the risk is still present, and perhaps 3000 people are seized, mutilated and, in most cases, eaten by crocodiles annually.

HUMANS AT RISK

The vast majority of victims are attacked by the Indo-Pacific crocodile (*Crocodylus porosus*), while the Nile crocodile (*Crocodylus niloticus*) is almost as dangerous. Perhaps not surprisingly, the number of human casualties involved far exceeds those taken by that great aquatic group

Plate 8   The narrow-snouted crocodilians are a group which feed primarily on fish, amphibians and other small vertebrates. Such crocodiles represent little danger to people, even when adult.

Plate 9 An Australian billabong – a typical habitat in Queensland where crocodiles may be encountered. Warnings are now posted in many areas, with the aim of avoiding conflict as crocodile populations rise, due to protective legislation.

of predators, the sharks. This is a direct reflection of the fact that human beings and crocodiles live in close proximity to each other.

In certain areas, however, attacks on people have been unusually

23

common. This can sometimes be traced back to some historical event, as in the case of Sesheke, a town on the Zambezi River. King Sepopo of the Barotse people regularly killed many prisoners here, by feeding them to the crocodiles in the river. King Sepopo was himself murdered in 1870, but the crocodiles retained their taste for human flesh and continued to plague Sesheke for decades afterwards.

Surprisingly few attempts have been made to protect people living in such areas from attacks. In parts of Angola, however, platforms have been constructed so that water can be obtained from the rivers without the risk of being seized by a crocodile.

In reality, only relatively large crocodilians, over 3 m ($9\frac{3}{4}$ ft) are likely to pose a threat to people. At this stage, they will normally start to take mammalian prey in the wild. The older they get, the more they turn to human beings, who are considered easier prey. Some man-eaters have been accused of killing up to 400 people, but this is probably a gross exaggeration.

There was a particularly gruesome incident during World War 2, however, when a big group of Indo-Pacific crocodiles slaughtered a large number of Japanese soldiers. This occurred during the British campaign to recapture Burma, when about 1000 retreating Japanese entered an area of mangrove swamp between Burma and Ramree Island, seeking the ships which were due to evacuate them.

A Royal Naval blockade left them trapped here as night came and the crocodiles moved in, with the slaughter continuing through the night. Finally, there were just 20 Japanese left alive. The vast majority had been killed by the crocodiles, although some drowned or may have been shot.

CROCODILIAN ATTACKS IN AUSTRALIA

In Australia, the Indo-Pacific crocodile is involved in the vast majority of attacks, whereas Johnston's crocodile *(Crocodylus johnstoni)* is generally considered to be inoffensive. This may be related to their feeding preferences, with Johnston's crocodile taking prey such as fish rather than mammals.

The Australian Aborigines recognize differences in the risk from various crocodile populations. In some areas, they maintain that even Indo-Pacific crocodiles will not attack them, and they venture into the water at these localities. Nevertheless, Aborigines do fall victim to crocodiles, often when wading in water.

Travellers venturing into parts of Australia where crocodiles are present are now often warned of their presence by signs at various localities. They are advised not to swim or wade in the water, and also to avoid camping nearby. Media interest in crocodilian attacks in Australia has increased considerably during recent years, and perhaps the most positive aspect of such coverage is that people are more aware of the risk.

Whether the reporting is accurate in all cases is doubtful, but it gave rise to many local legends, with none becoming better known than the case of the Indo-Pacific crocodile christened 'Sweetheart'. The attacks were recorded in the area of water known locally as Sweet's Billabong, part of the Finniss River system. The term 'billabong' refers to a branch of a river which comes to a dead end, and Sweet's Billabong measured about 9 km ($5\frac{1}{2}$ miles) in length and up to 100 m (109 yd) across at its widest point.

This stretch of water was known locally to be the home of several large crocodiles. The first known attack took place at night during 1974, when a boat with three people on board was seized and shaken by a crocodile. One person was thrown into the water, but luckily scrambled back without injury. The crocodile then attacked the propeller as the party tried to reach land. A more serious attack occurred two years later, when the crocodile's teeth actually penetrated the aluminium hull of a boat.

In all cases, boats were the target of the crocodile's aggression, with such incidents becoming more frequent during 1978, when the crocodile savaged an outboard motor on a moored boat and then managed to sink another boat. The two occupants were able to swim to safety while the giant reptile continued to attack the boat. A similar attack took place in the following year and prompted official action.

It was decided to capture the crocodile concerned, before any further incidents led to fatalities. Finally, during July 1979, after much effort, this was achieved using a special trap. Unfortunately, Sweetheart, who weighed in at 780 kg (1720 lb), and measured 5.1 m (17 ft) from snout to tail, did not survive for long after capture and died, probably because of the stress involved. His remains are now prominently displayed in the Northern Territory Museum at Darwin.

Another case similar to that of Sweetheart occurred during May and June 1984, in a billabong which formed part of the Wildman River, also in the Northern Territory. This crocodile again attacked boats and, similarly, died soon after being caught.

Clearly, there is something about craft with outboard motors attached which leads the crocodiles to behave in this way, and various explanations have been put forward. The first clue came from a bushman, who told how crocodiles would ignore a stick placed near them unless it had been heated in a fire, in which case they would attack it, having detected its warmth.

Plate 10   Airboats are widely used to study crocodilian populations in localities as far apart as Florida, USA, and Northern Territory, Australia. They are ideal for travelling through relatively shallow water, but problems may arise if there is a breakdown, as Hilton Graham discovered. It nearly cost him his life.

Graham Webb, who has spent many years studying Indo-Pacific crocodiles, discovered that the appearance of the outboard motor's propeller in the water is rather similar to the head of an animal. The crocodiles could therefore have seen the boat as potential prey, and aimed to strike at what they perceived to be its most vulnerable point.

In addition, the frequency of the sound emitted from the propeller of an outboard falls within the range of that produced by Indo-Pacific crocodiles. In other words, Sweetheart may have viewed the boats as potential rivals, invading his territory, and so attacked them. This explanation is probably the most plausible because, even when there were people in the water, Sweetheart ignored them, continuing with his assault on their boats.

Breeding crocodiles may well be more aggressive towards people than usual. This is confirmed by a study of attacks on people by Nile crocodiles, carried out in the region of northern Zululand and southern Mozambique. Thirty-nine of the 43 documented attacks in this area took place during the breeding period, from November to early April.

Back in Australia, nesting Indo-Pacific crocodiles are said to be equally dangerous. It was thought that a breeding female attacked lecturer Valerie Plumwood on the East Alligator River during February 1985. She was in a canoe, and saw the crocodile, which was over 3 m ($9\frac{3}{4}$ ft) in length, before it turned on her. The canoe became grounded and the crocodile attacked the craft and then turned on Valerie as she scrambled to escape up the river bank. It followed and lunged at her again. Luckily, in spite of being seriously injured, she survived.

26

Plate 11   In Florida, particularly, a growing number of alligator attacks on people and pets are being reported. The authorities operate a nuisance alligator scheme to deal with such cases.

Plate 12   Education is playing a major part in alligator territory in the south of the USA. Residents and visitors alike are being asked to view alligators as an integral part of the natural environment. But this does not extend to permitting the feeding of alligators, because of the danger that the alligator will ultimately bite the hand which feeds it.

Graham Webb is another person who can testify to the aggression of female crocodiles when guarding their nesting sites. He was examining a nest on the Adelaide River, to the east of Darwin, when the concealed female attacked him in shallow water. Webb was lucky to escape with just a severe laceration to his leg.

One of the tragedies in a number of other documented attacks in Australia is that alcohol has encouraged people to take risks which would be inconceivable in the cold, sober light of day. Swimming at night in areas infested by crocodiles is particularly dangerous. But this did not deter Paul Flanagan, who had apparently been drinking, from swimming close to the blood drain from the Wyndham meat-processing plant in Western Australia. A large number of crocodiles was known to congregate in this stretch of water and, on the following day, Flanagan's badly mauled body was found upstream near where he had last been seen on a sandbank.

The likelihood of escaping (even if entirely sober) from an attack by a large crocodile is not good. But some remarkable tales of survival have been documented. One of the most noteworthy involved Hilton Graham, who was working at the time as a safari operator, and Peta Lynn Mann, the daughter of his partner. They were in an airboat to the north of the Daly River in the Northern Territory, when the machine went aground in shallow water.

Graham jumped out to free it and lost his revolver in the water. As he bent to retrieve it, he caught a glimpse of an Indo-Pacific crocodile, which lunged at him. In the struggle that followed, he battled ferociously with the 4 m (13 ft) reptile and, possibly by gouging at its eyes, he was able to break free, although it left his arm shattered.

When Graham tried to scramble to the bank, the crocodile renewed its attack, grabbing him this time around the thigh and buttocks. It started to drag him towards deeper water, where the outcome of the struggle would inevitably have been fatal.

But Peta Lynn Mann bravely clung on to Graham's arm and managed to keep hold of him. The crocodile, having inflicted awful wounds on Graham, then relinquished its grip and disappeared. Later, Peta personally received a bravery award from Queen Elizabeth II for her efforts, while Hilton Graham, after a long and painful period of convalescence, ironically turned to a new career – crocodile farming.

CROCODILIAN ATTACKS IN THE AMERICAS

Although the American alligator (*Alligator mississippiensis*) is often considered to be dangerous, these reptiles are actually much more placid than either the Nile or Indo-Pacific crocodiles. This view is confirmed by zookeepers who have experience of all three species. Between 1948 and 1971, for example, there were probably less than ten unprovoked attacks by alligators in the state of Florida, with no fatalities recorded. In all instances, it appears that the alligators did not distinguish between people and their normal prey, but rapidly abandoned their interest once their intended victims fought back.

The situation in Florida may be changing to some extent, however, as the state becomes an ever more popular retirement and holiday area. There is an increasing demand for waterfront properties and this has inevitably led to greater conflict with alligators in the region. The numbers of these reptiles has also increased considerably in Florida, as they have been protected here since the early 1970s. As a result, from 1973 to 1988, the number of attacks by alligators on people rose to 90 and, in five cases, people were killed.

In an attempt to reduce this problem, the Florida Game and Fresh Water Fish Commission has sought to educate the public about alligators and their habits. Even so, they receive about 7000 complaints each year concerning alligators. Many of these stem from the presence of the reptiles in pools on the lawns of houses and even in the water holes around golf courses. In response, the Commission removes about 3000 alligators annually from such places, to lessen the risk of conflict, although they try to impress on complainants that, ultimately, the alligator will retreat on its own.

By way of contrast, some people actively encourage alligators and may try to feed them on scraps. This is a dangerous practice, because the reptiles soon lose their normal sense of fear and then may even start to pursue people in search of food. As a result, the feeding of alligators in Florida has been outlawed, as, of course, is either killing or disturbing the creatures.

One of the major aims of the Commission's campaign is to convince both residents and visitors alike that people and alligators can peacefully co-exist, emphasizing the fact that these reptiles are an integral part of the Florida wetlands. By designating safe swimming areas for people and pets, the Commission attempts to prevent any possible conflicts of interest.

In reality, however, with nearly half a million visitors coming to the Everglades National Park every year, the number of attacks reported throughout the state is minuscule, although swimming alongside alligators remains exceedingly dangerous. Alligators are highly adept at remaining concealed until their potential prey is within reach, and so can strike a person or pet dog totally unexpectedly.

The American crocodile (*Crocodylus acutus*), although far less common than the alligator, can also be potentially dangerous. One unpleasant incident involving this species took place during 1925, at Biscayne Bay, close to Miami in Florida. The crocodile in question was shot by a surveyor, and appeared dead, but when one of his group kicked the reptile, it swung its tail round, knocked the man over and then killed him as he lay on the ground.

This crocodile was then taken off to an alligator farm, before being passed to Ross Allen's famous Reptile Institute. Here, somewhat ironically, the man-eater lived to old age, finally succumbing in a fight with a big alligator which was housed in the neighbouring enclosure. On its death in 1953, it was estimated to have been at least 65 years old.

There are few other documented attacks by this species, although, in some parts of Mexico, these reptiles may prove dangerous when women and children wash in local rivers. Similar accounts originate from other parts of Central America as well, but clearly the American crocodile is not a particularly aggressive species.

South American crocodilians are also rarely pugnacious towards people, with the possible exception of the black caiman (*Melanosuchus niger*). The Orinoco crocodile (*Crocodylus intermedius*) may also occasionally resort to taking human prey, but again, there are very few documented cases.

THE MISJUDGED GHARIAL OF INDIA

After a fatal attack, people in an area will often seek to kill the crocodilian responsible. This is carried out obviously for revenge in some cases, but also to prevent the crocodilian concerned from acquiring a taste for human flesh.

The remains of the unfortunate victim are often recovered from inside the crocodilian. But the mere presence of parts of the body and jewellery in the crocodilian's tract is not clear evidence that it is a killer of people. The gharial (*Gavialis gangeticus*) used to be viewed as a dangerous species, until it was realized that the human remains in its body originated from Indian funeral practices. The remains are tipped into the river, and so the gharials were in fact scavenging on the corpses. Other crocodilians in the region, including the mugger (*Crocodylus palustris*) and even the notorious Indo-Pacific crocodile, may also obtain some of their food by this means. A Malay proverb, describing how some people will take advantage of any situation, actually reflects this habit by asking 'When will a crocodile refuse a corpse?'

RECOVERY FROM ATTACK

Overall, the incidence of crocodilians attacking people is undoubtedly low, even amongst the species which are known to be most aggressive. Hugh Cott, who studied the stomach contents of the Nile crocodile, noted that out of 444 large specimens which he shot, only four of these crocodilians had human remains in their stomachs.

Unfortunately, convalescence from a crocodile attack can be a lengthy and medically demanding period. In more primitive parts of the world, subsequent mortality from septicaemia is likely. Part of this problem may result from the sharp, pointed shape of the crocodile's teeth, which inject pathogenic bacteria deep within the victim's muscle. In addition, the force with which the teeth slice through the flesh causes tissue necrosis, establishing favourable conditions for ana- erobic bacterial infections, which can be resistant to antibiotics. Even a relatively small bite should therefore receive prompt medical attention and it may take several months to heal properly.

HUNTING CROCODILIANS

Before modern weapons, crocodile hunting was a dangerous pursuit. In various parts of the world, these reptiles were caught with a reinforced form of a hook and line. Probably because of the risks involved, hunts were often linked with elaborate rituals and incantations to ensure a

Plate 13   The dorsal armour of the crocodilian is especially well developed and often able to withstand the impact of primitive spears. But the advent of modern firearms has proved to have a more dramatic effect on their numbers than any other single event in their long history.

successful outcome. This applied especially if the crocodile concerned was believed to have killed people previously.

In Borneo, the hunting of such crocodiles is the responsibility of the local witch-doctor, who is paid for this work by the grieving family. Once he has been hired, the witch-doctor will rely on the generosity of others to feed him while he prepares for the task ahead. By tradition, he must swallow this food without chewing it, rather like the crocodile itself. Based at a hut close to where the victim was taken, the witch-doctor sets out in a small red and yellow boat, with lances that can be used to spear the crocodile. The selection of suitable bait for the hook is a complex matter, based on the drawing of lots to determine the most auspicious.

Having caught and killed a crocodile, the witch-doctor will then examine its stomach contents for any evidence that it was a man-eater. He continues killing crocodiles in this fashion until one is discovered. This then becomes a cause for celebration, and the remaining crocodiles are pacified by being offered a cat, to show that they were not the hunter's target.

Various special traps have been devised for catching crocodiles in different parts of the world. The Seminole Indians of North America used two converging lines of stout branches set in the shallow water near the alligators' usual haunts. At the far end of the trap, there was an 'S'-shaped bend, and here meat or fish were placed as a bait. Once an alligator had entered the trap, it then found itself unable to back out because of the sigmoid flexure, and it could either be killed, or left until required for a meal.

In Pakistan, a more perilous means of catching crocodiles as a source of food used to be practised by the Sind tribe. A group of men pursued a crocodile by paddling on copper floats, called *dillos*. Their buoyancy came from air trapped in the vessel by the hunter lying across the hole on the *dillos*'s upper surface. Armed with nets and poles, the men would aim to surround the reptile, so that it burrowed into the mud on the floor of the river.

By careful probing, they could establish its position and would rapidly drive the bamboo poles into the river bed on each side of its body. Then, with the struggling crocodile trapped, two divers would loop a stout rope around its body under water. It could then be pulled out of the water, while being restrained by the surrounding nets if it attempted to break free. Once on land, the crocodile was traditionally killed with long-handled axes.

Crocodilians are actually well protected by their body armour against a direct physical attack. Spearing these reptiles is therefore difficult but the ancient Greek writer, Pliny, described a tribe of African pygmies who hunted Nile crocodiles by ramming a sharp wooden spear directly into the back of their mouths. Similar hunting methods are employed by various tribespeople around the world today.

The killing of crocodiles was revolutionized during the nineteenth century by the development of reliable, powerful firearms, whose bullets could penetrate the protective casing of the crocodilian's body. Prior to this, firearms could not be relied upon to dispatch a crocodile effectively, largely because of their low muzzle velocity.

Crocodilians soon became a popular target for big-game hunters, seeking trophies of their travels. In the USA it even became fashionable to shoot alligators from river boats plying up and down the major waterways. As a result, by the turn of the century, these crocodilians had become very scarce in such localities.

CROCODILIANS IN COMMERCE

THE TRADE IN ALLIGATOR SKINS IN THE USA

By this time, a considerable trade in alligator skins had started to develop, the leather being used for a wide array of items, from footwear to bags and belts. It is hard to obtain a reliable overall picture of this trade, but it certainly developed to the point where, in some areas, it threatened the survival of the species.

Within the USA, New York State became the major centre for the worldwide distribution of alligator skins, with as many as 60,000 being sold here by individual firms each year. The total figure for the industry may have been near 300,000. The majority of alligators involved originated from Florida, although those from Louisiana were considered to yield skins of a better quality.

The tanners encountered problems with the Florida skins, because of the presence of so-called 'corn marks', caused by hard tissue within the belly scutes. The Key West population was deemed the worst in this respect, although having a longer body than those from elsewhere, Florida's alligators were still sought after for the manufacture of big handbags. For smaller articles, such as wallets, the skin from Louisiana alligators was preferable, because of its more attractive appearance.

The demand became so great that not only did the populations of the American crocodile suffer as well, but a thriving trade built up in skins obtained from parts of both Central and South America. There was little, if any, attempt to distinguish between the species, however, and all such products carried an alligator tag. By 1902, it is estimated that half of the 280,000 crocodilian hides being processed in the USA originated from elsewhere in the Americas.

Plate 14   It is the belly skin which determines the commercial value of a crocodilian species, although, within individual populations, there may be some variation. The Key West alligators, for example, had bony osteoderms on the belly, which dramatically reduced the appeal of their hide for the tanneries.

Such a vast trade was clearly not sustainable. Figures suggest that at least $2\frac{1}{2}$ million alligators were slaughtered in Florida for the leather business during the last century, and from 1880 to 1933 alone, about $3\frac{1}{2}$ million were slaughtered in Louisiana. Hunting conditions here were particularly good during the mid-1920s, when there was a severe drought.

The declining population of alligators can be traced through sales' records. In 1929, approximately 190,000 hides were traded in Florida, with the best grade selling for US \$1.50. Within five years, the number on offer had fallen by about a third, with the price doubling from its 1929 level. A decade later, there were only 80,000 skins obtained and the price stood at US \$5.25.

By 1943, it was clear that drastic action was needed to safeguard the remaining populations, when just 6800 hides were available to buyers. In the following year, a ban on hunting during the breeding period was introduced, and young alligators less than 1.2 m (4 ft) long became

34

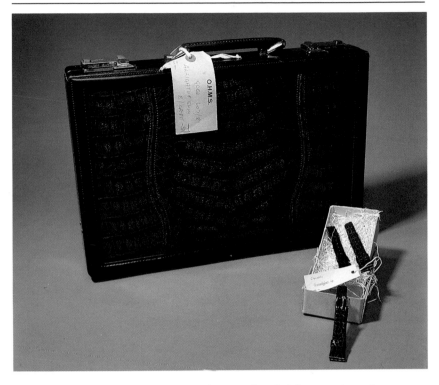

Plate 15   Although crocodile-skin products, such as briefcases and watchstraps, can be sold legally, moving them internationally may create problems unless they are accompanied by the correct paperwork. These are examples confiscated from travellers entering the UK. Proper documentation is vital to ensure the leather does not originate from an endangered wild population.

fully protected by law. The benefits of these measures became clear within three years. In 1947, the number of hides obtained had risen to 25,000, and this was reflected by a decline in price, down from a peak of US $19.25 in 1943 to an average of US $13.30.

Finally, during 1961, the hunting of alligators was made illegal in Florida, but this simply led to an upsurge in poaching. Federal legislation, achieved through an amendment to the Lacey Act, meant that alligator hides could no longer be moved across state lines, since the alligator was a protected species, and this curbed the activities of poachers. Four years later, in 1973, the federal Endangered Species Act gave mandatory protection to crocodiles and alligators throughout the USA.

In Florida today, alligators have recolonized much of what remains of their former territories and are not normally hunted. Louisiana, however, has sought to utilize these reptiles on a sustainable yield basis, with a programme which began in 1972. Enforcement is achieved by means of a series of controls, including licences and tags, backed by annual monitoring of the alligator population in the state.

This is carried out partly by aerial surveys of the nesting sites in the coastal marsh areas. Elsewhere, population estimates are made relying on data obtained in night counts. The method used entails observations of the eyes of alligators in the water, which reflect back the light of a torch making them easy to count accurately. Information obtained from skin sizes also gives valuable insight into the population dynamics in an area. As a rather literal interpretation of this methodology, if there are few large alligators, then it is reasonable to assume that excessive hunting has taken place during previous years.

There are still various controls on the killing of alligators within areas where hunting them is permitted. Hunting at night, for example, when alligators may be easily identified by using a flashlight to illuminate their eyes, is outlawed. By controlling the hunting season, the hunting method and the areas where hunting may take place, it has proved possible to regulate the catch, in terms of taking males rather than the females, which are of greater significance to the overall population.

The majority of skins fall within the range of 1.5–2.4 m (5–8 ft) in length. Using a computer system it is now possible to track the individual skins through to the tannery. These are sold throughout the world, to buyers as far afield as Japan, France and Italy, and in a ten-year period, the harvest has comprised over 100,000 alligators in total.

A particularly encouraging feature of this programme is that the alligator population of Louisiana is now maintained at a level just below that which existed at the end of the last century. Working with contemporary trade data from that period, it has proved possible to gain a reliable understanding of the numbers of alligators then found in Louisiana.

The flesh of alligators is a further important by-product of the skin harvest. Alligators had traditionally been eaten in North America by native Americans, long before the advent of European settlers. Their meat is said by its devotees to taste rather like a cross between lobster and chicken when cooked, and it still finds a ready market in Louisiana, where there are various traditional recipes for alligator dishes. Recently, alligator meat has also been exported, and it appears on the menus of gourmet restaurants in London and elsewhere. This is in sharp contrast to the situation in the last century, when slaves were regularly fed alligator tails, which were considered to be a cheap source of protein.

Teeth also have a value, being sold as curios or for the jewellery trade. This business is centred on the city of New Orleans. But in spite of the clear commercial value of the American alligator in Louisiana, it is evident that there is no major illegal trade in this species.

As in Florida, there is also a nuisance alligator programme, which permits the killing of animals which are proving a problem in a specific area, if they cannot be moved elsewhere for whatever reason. Tags are used to identify the skins of such alligators before they enter the trade, and these remain in place throughout the actual tanning process.

THE CROCODILE TRADE IN AUSTRALIA

During the early years of European settlement in Australia, crocodiles were killed for sport, but much of their habitat remained inaccessible. Trade in crocodile skins had begun in a small way around the turn of the century, possibly stimulated by the demand for alligator hides in the USA, but it did not prove very successful.

It was only much later, beginning in the 1940s, that hunters set out in earnest to obtain skins, often venturing into remote and previously largely unexplored areas of the country. Crocodiles could be plentiful here, with up to 15 per kilometre of river (1100 yd) being reported in some parts of the Northern Territory, but in many cases, their densities were much lower. The majority were to be found not in tidal rivers, but rather in freshwater areas surrounded by swampland. By the end of the decade, those that inhabited tidal rivers had been largely eliminated by overhunting.

The hunting effort at this stage was directed almost entirely towards the Indo-Pacific crocodile, with the Aborigines playing a key role in such expeditions. Their knowledge of the areas and hunting skills were critical to the success of these operations.

As demand increased, so hunters were forced to turn some of their attention to the freshwater Johnston's crocodile (*Crocodylus johnstoni*) at the end of the 1950s. Indo-Pacific crocodiles were becoming scarce and, with improvements in the tanning process, it became feasible to use the skins from Johnston's crocodiles. Up until this stage, the presence of bony plates (osteoderms) meant that such skins had previously been regarded as being of inferior quality.

It also proved considerably easier to trap Johnston's crocodiles since, during the dry season, they would congregate in groups. Trawling billabongs with nets guaranteed a good catch, but could clearly threaten the survival of this endemic Australian species. Amid growing concern, Western Australia introduced protective legislation in 1962, followed by the Northern Territory during the following year.

Unfortunately, the third state with a population of these crocodiles, Queensland, did not follow suit until 1974. This enabled widespread

37

Plate 16   The demise of large crocodiles in Australia left the hunters with little
hope of income. They turned to marketing youngsters as curios and this trade
flourishes today, as these grotesque specimens illustrate.

killing to continue in remote parts of the other states, with the hunters
then marketing the skins as being legally obtained in Queensland.

Crocodile hunters in Australia eliminated their quarry to the point
when they could no longer earn a living. Throughout much of its
range, the Indo-Pacific crocodile had declined drastically. Hatchlings
could still be obtained, often caught on a hook and line, and these were
mounted as grotesque objects for the tourist trade.

The damage had been done. It is estimated that about 270,000
Indo-Pacific crocodile skins were obtained over a 27-year period,
beginning in 1945. A similar number of Johnston's crocodiles were also
killed for the skin trade. But a key factor in their subsequent recovery

Plate 17   Tourism is now coming to the aid of the crocodilian. Visitors to alligator farms in Florida may buy from a wide range of suitably safe souvenirs to remind them, at least temporarily in this case, of their visit. Asia's largest crocodile farm now attracts over one million tourists annually, confirming that crocodilians can indeed become big business while alive.

was that their actual range had not been dramatically reduced. Although very scarce in some areas, sufficient crocodiles remained to form a breeding population, and, with their habitat intact, these could increase in numbers.

But crocodile populations in Australia have still not fully recovered, in spite of legal protection, to their 1930s levels. Johnston's crocodile appears to have increased faster in numbers than the Indo-Pacific species, possibly because it suffered a shorter hunting period. In addition, the areas where Johnston's crocodile are found are generally more remote, and here they face less disturbance today.

HUNTING AND TRADE ELSEWHERE IN THE WORLD

Crocodile hunting in Africa has a long history, dating back to at least the middle of the last century. The *Natal Herald*, in 1869, noted the great demand which had developed for crocodile leather. In Europe at the time, it was particularly popular for ladies' boots, because of its soft and pliable nature. This triggered an interest in commercial hunting, although the numbers of crocodiles taken are unclear.

Certainly it appears that crocodiles remained numerous in spite of this pressure, because, in Natal, around the turn of the century, the government was offering a substantial bounty for each dead crocodile brought in to a magistrate's office, as well as for their eggs. Hunters earned substantial sums during the early 1900s from this attempt to eradicate crocodiles as pests. Strychnine baits were used to lure the reptiles to their deaths, proving a safe if not ecologically sound hunting method for those involved.

The widespread killing of crocodiles for the skin trade developed quite late in southern Africa, although by the 1930s, there were professional hunters active in the region. Their annual individual take appears to have been around 100 crocodiles. But the industry really began to grow after World War 2. Although claims of individual hunters killing up to 45,000 crocodiles are probably exaggerated, it is certainly clear that, within the course of little more than two decades, the numbers of Nile crocodiles had shrunk drastically in Africa. Up to 3 million may have been killed and other species were probably also affected, but to a lesser extent.

As one example of their decline, during an expedition to Angola in 1953, crocodiles were not sighted at all in the Cuanza River, where previously considerable numbers had occurred, and only one individual was seen in the nearby Cubal River. Hunters had aimed to wipe out all crocodiles in an area before moving on to eliminate further populations.

Regulation was relatively slow in coming, but again, in some parts of their range, especially away from human settlements, the numbers of Nile crocodiles have subsequently increased. In Natal itself, within the Ndumu Game Reserve, an Experimental Crocodile Research and Restocking Station was established to assist in the recovery process. Over a 13-year period, beginning in 1966, it began to release young crocodiles back into areas where they had formerly been numerous.

Enforcement of hunting bans is often difficult to achieve, especially for species which are perceived to be a threat to human existence, and with only small budgets for policing purposes. In French Guiana, for example, where the black caiman (*Melanosuchus niger*) is protected, it is apparently not unusual for some crocodilians offered for sale in the food markets to have their heads removed. Without this identifying feature, it is virtually impossible to tell the difference between the protected black caiman and the common caiman (*Caiman crocodilus*), which may be legitimately traded.

The reason for the decline of the black caiman can be traced back to the 1950s, when it was ruthlessly hunted for its skin. Prior to this, the crocodiles of the Orinoco basin had been heavily slaughtered during the 1930s by prisoners who had escaped in French Guiana. They sought their quarry after dark, harpooning the crocodilians and then selling the skins.

Following the demise of these other species, hunting in South America today is now concentrated on the common caiman, especially in the Pantanal area of Brazil. In spite of national protection, the trade in the skins of these crocodilians is widespread and carried out on a large scale. Curios made from hatchlings, such as key-rings featuring a young caiman's head as their fob, still find a market in Europe and elsewhere.

Species with a restricted range are most vulnerable to the effects of intensive hunting. Indeed, the Philippine crocodile (*Crocodylus mindorensis*) has been pushed to the verge of extinction following widespread killing of populations throughout its range. It also faces increasing development of its habitat. Similarly, the Siamese crocodile (*Crocodylus siamensis*) had virtually been exterminated by the early 1970s, as the result of uncontrolled hunting pressures.

In Papua New Guinea, the Indo-Pacific crocodile was the original target of the expatriates who began the skin trade here in the late 1940s. At this time, these crocodiles were quite numerous but, as their numbers declined, so it was left to the natives to venture into the remote regions where some still survived. The expatriates running the industry switched from hunting to purchasing and marketing the skins which the natives obtained.

A reduction in the size of skins, as older animals were eliminated, and a declining catch meant that, by the late 1960s, attention had moved on from the Indo-Pacific species to the endemic New Guinea crocodile (*Crocodylus novaeguineae*). This smaller species accounted for over 90 per cent of the skin trade at this stage, with the consequent elimination of whole populations. It disappeared from parts of the Fly River and, even where it had been numerous, in the vicinity of Lake Murray for example, the New Guinea crocodile vanished almost totally because of the hunting pressures.

Again, official action to protect these species appears to have been slow, but the results are now encouraging. Beginning in 1977, a programme was established to reward the native people for catching juvenile crocodiles which could be used in recognized breeding units. The decline in the population of the New Guinea crocodile had directly affected the tribespeople of the interior because it was an important item of food for them. Now, with greater awareness of the situation, the numbers of both species of crocodilian found in Papua New Guinea are currently rising again.

CROCODILIAN RANCHING AND FARMING

The keeping of crocodilians in enclosures dates back centuries, with the 'mugger-peer' of Karachi, on the Indian sub-continent, being one of the most famous. It appears to have much in common with the ancient

Plate 18   Gator farms capitalize on the reproductive capacity of the female alligator. In the wild, if 45 eggs are laid, the majority of hatchlings die at an early stage. But in a controlled environment, a very high percentage of the youngsters can be reared satisfactorily and, ultimately, their hides and meat can be sold.

Egyptian crocodile ponds at Tebtunis. The forehead of the largest of the crocodiles here was decorated with red. It lived on its own, while the others shared a communal area.

Although now considered to be of primary importance for tourists, this collection of crocodiles had a potent religious significance in the past. The crocodiles were believed to be the servants of Vishnu, who created water, and so were highly venerated. Indeed, villages throughout the sub-continent often kept a crocodile for this reason.

Today, in many parts of the world where crocodilians occur, they are being kept in increasing numbers, not for religious reasons, but for commercial and conservation purposes. In the early 1900s, it was possible for tourists to visit so-called crocodile ranches and view a number of these reptiles on display. But serious attempts at breeding and rearing crocodilians in captivity did not commence until the 1960s, when it was clear that a number of species were in serious decline. Farming crocodilians was perceived as a means of ensuring their survival and the survival of the skin trade which had brought various species to the verge of extinction.

Since then, there has been a number of significant moves within the conservation community to encourage the development of a sustainable harvest of crocodilian skins. The founding of the Convention on International Trade in Endangered Species (CITES) in 1973 has led

Plate 19   High stocking densities can usually be achieved with no detrimental effects, although, obviously, management practices must be sound in such surroundings, because otherwise disease can spread rapidly.

Plate 20   A novel means of moving young alligators safely is practised here in Florida, with the tubes full of the reptiles being transported if necessary on flat-back lorries.

to the encouragement of quota controls on wild crocodilians, backed by field studies, and on-going farming and ranching projects, as well as trade bans on endangered species.

There is a significant difference between a ranch and a farm, because ranching entails the use of wild-caught stock. Eggs, hatchlings or adults from the wild may be involved in a ranching operation. The eggs or hatchlings form the basis of rearing projects, whereby young crocodilians are grown to a marketable size and then killed. Adults are taken in accordance with a quota and their skins are traded under strict controls.

A true crocodile farm is, by definition, a closed breeding unit, which is not reliant on the acquisition of eggs or animals from the wild, although, in some cases, additional genetic input from this source may be authorized. For CITES purposes, it is necessary for a farm to show that the species kept have been bred to the second (F2) generation.

There are a number of factors which make crocodilians ideal subjects for ranching and farming purposes. In the first instance, they have a relatively high reproductive potential, with females frequently laying more than 30 eggs per clutch. In the wild, relatively few hatchlings

Plate 21   Labelling of crocodilian products, as undertaken here by the Conservation Commission of Northern Territory, Australia, confirms the validity of the goods concerned, by disclosing their origins. Such trade is becoming increasingly vital to the well-being of crocodilian populations in many areas.

survive to maturity, so numbers can be removed for ranching purposes without harming the status of the overall population. It would be far more damaging to remove reproductively mature females.

Young crocodilians will grow rapidly if housed and fed properly, and it is possible to rear them under fairly intensive conditions. The quality of the skins from ranched crocodilians also tends to be more uniform. Such projects offer employment to native people and help to prevent poaching of wild populations, as well as being easier to regulate. There is also considerable incentive for people to protect breeding crocodiles in the wild since, without these, ranching will no longer be possible.

A secondary, but no less vital contribution made by these enterprises to the conservation of crocodilians is the large amount of information obtained concerning the reproductive biology, nutritional needs and health status of these reptiles. There is also a potential for tourism in some areas, as well as sales of meat and other by-products.

A number of logistical requirements have to be met before a ranch or farm can be established. The area concerned must have an adequate supply of water available throughout the year, to supply the holding ponds. If pumping facilities need to be established, this will entail not only additional expense, but also proper maintenance.

A readily available source of fish or meat to feed the crocodilians is also essential for the success of the enterprise. This may come from a local abbatoir or from shrimp fishermen. In some instances, fish, notably the cichlid *Tilapia*, are reared for this purpose.

IN THE INDO-PACIFIC

In Papua New Guinea, crocodile ranching began during 1972 and has received international support from United Nations' agencies. There are now about 300 operations of this type and government loans are available to establish such enterprises. Some are small-scale businesses, operated at village level. These typically comprise a single pen, fenced using posts set 60 cm (2 ft) below ground and about 1.5 m (5 ft) high, so that the crocodiles cannot escape. There is a pool near the centre of the enclosure, which is shaded with trees and grasses, providing a retreat for the crocodiles away from direct sunlight.

These small-scale units often do not rear the crocodiles to maturity. Instead, they are collecting points for larger operations, which hold up to 1000 crocodiles. These have a series of enclosures, around 6 m² (20 ft²) and are sometimes located close to an airstrip. From here, the young crocodiles may ultimately be taken to one of the main farms, such as that at Lae, on the northern coast. This unit accommodates around 8000 crocodiles, on a 100-ha (247-acre) site, adjacent to a

Plate 22   Not all farming or ranching enterprises are carried out on a large scale. The ranching scheme that has operated in Papua New Guinea since 1972 ranges from a simple village base up to a sophisticated unit holding many thousands of crocodilians. Access to adequate supplies of water and food throughout the year is critical for success.

poultry slaughterhouse. They are reared and fed on the waste from this plant.

In addition to the skins, the meat produced on this farm is both sold locally and exported. With an average carcass yielding up to 20 kg (44 lb) for human consumption, the supply of crocodile meat means that Papua New Guinea has to spend less of its valuable foreign exchange on importing other meat. The meat is also low in fat, and this may trigger further overseas sales, as people in Europe become more health-conscious regarding their diet.

Alongside commercial farms, the government has also established demonstration units, where those interested in crocodile ranching can come and learn the techniques. The success of the programme is reflected by the fact that, within ten years of its inception, farms held stocks of 30,000 crocodiles, guaranteeing a production of around 10,000 skins per annum.

Indonesia has also established a number of crocodile-rearing units for commercial production, located primarily in Irian Jaya, the western part of New Guinea. In 1989 there were about 19,000 crocodiles

Plate 23   The use of poultry carcasses or fish to form the basis of a crocodilian's diet may be superseded by specific rations, as shown here. This prepared food can be purchased in bulk and, provided that it is kept dry and away from vermin, will not deteriorate. Units, in remote areas of Australia for example, may benefit from this approach.

here, but as elsewhere, the viability of such ranches depends on various financial factors, and not all are in continuous production.

The most successful ranching and breeding enterprise in Asia is located in Thailand. The Samutprakan Crocodile Farm was founded here, south of Bangkok, in 1950. Since then, it has grown to become one of the largest in the world, maintaining an average stock of 30,000 crocodilians. The majority of these are kept for their skins, but there is also a separate breeding unit, comprising about 4000 crocodilians.

The native Thai species, the Indo-Pacific and Siamese crocodiles, predominate on the farm, but other species are also seen here, often in large open-air pools. These include the false gavial (*Tomistoma schlegelii*), which also occurs in Thailand, as well as the Chinese alligator (*Alligator sinensis*), New Guinea crocodile (*Crocodylus novaeguineae*) and several species of caiman.

The Samutprakan Crocodile Farm has subsequently become a major tourist attraction since opening its gates to visitors in 1971. It now entertains one million tourists each year, who can watch novelty crocodile wrestling, as well as the more usual features of a farm. About 5 tonnes of fish are used daily to feed the crocodilians here, with any shortfall being made up using poultry offal.

Not all farms are geared for commercial production of skins however. Indeed, the Samutprakan Crocodile Farm has itself also played a

47

major role in ensuring the survival of the Siamese crocodile. It was following the first meeting of the International Union for the Conservation of Nature and Natural Resources' (IUCN) Crocodile Specialist Group in New York, that the decision was taken to establish a collection of the world's crocodilians, as a gene bank to ensure their future survival. Four years later, in 1975, the first steps towards this goal were taken with the opening of the Madras Crocodile Bank in India. From a small start with just 14 muggers (*Crocodylus palustris*), there are now 10 species kept here, comprising about 3500 individuals.

Considerable research, both in the laboratory and field, is carried out, supported by international funding. Here also, tourists are a priority, with the 3.5-ha ($8\frac{1}{2}$-acre) site attracting half a million visitors each year. Surplus crocodilians from the breeding programme have been used in reintroduction schemes, backed by a public education policy. It is planned that species not presently in the collection at Madras will be added in the near future, completing part of the original goal of the IUCN Crocodile Specialist Group.

Other conservation-orientated crocodile units have been established in China and the Philippines. At Xuancheng, in Anhui Province, China, a farm has been set up for Chinese alligators (*Alligator sinensis*). This species is not favoured by the leather trade because of the relatively large number of osteoderms on its ventral skin, but, nevertheless, it has still declined quite dramatically in the wild during recent years.

Similarly, on Negros Island in the Philippines, a breeding project has been started at Silliman University in Dumaguete City. This is catering for the endangered Philippine crocodile (*Crocodylus mindorensis*), and a number have already been bred here. A pair of 3-year-olds of this species were released in the Calawit National Park in northern Busuanga. It is hoped that these in turn will breed in the area, where suitable protected habitat remains for them.

IN AUSTRALIA

The Australian crocodile farming industry, which now numbers eight farms or ranches in total, began directly as the result of welfare concerns. In 1969 there was considerable alarm about the numbers of Indo-Pacific hatchling crocodiles which were being killed in the State of Queensland for the curio trade. It was decided to try to prevent this slaughter by purchasing the hatchlings alive from hunters and rearing them on a farm.

The unit was sited at the Edward River Aboriginal Community, on the Cape York Peninsula of Queensland. Although about 600 baby crocodiles were received, the majority were in such bad condition that they were simply released in the locality, in the hope that some might survive in these surroundings.

Then, backed by the Commonwealth Department of Aboriginal Affairs, it was decided to redevelop the farm as a breeding and rearing unit in 1976. Permits were issued which enabled 49 Indo-Pacific crocodiles bigger than 2.8 m (9 ft) to be taken in order to start the programme.

Unfortunately, the remote location of this farm has meant that obtaining adequate food supplies, especially during the wet season when roads are often impassable, can be a problem. Nevertheless, the enterprise has flourished and now there are nearly 8000 crocodiles here, the vast majority of which have been bred on site.

The industry in Australia is centred on Queensland and the Northern Territory, with all four farms in the former state being breeding units rather than ranches. In the Northern Territory, there is a specific management plan which authorizes the collection of a maximum of 4000 Indo-Pacific crocodile eggs from the areas of the Finniss-Reynolds River system and from the Adelaide River. Also, 2000 Johnston's crocodile eggs can be taken, and it is clear from constant monitoring that this collection policy is having no detrimental effects on the populations here. The farms also play a useful role in taking crocodiles which have become a problem in certain areas and would otherwise have to be shot.

As a relative latecomer to crocodilian captive management programmes, Australia has drawn on the experiences of other countries, including its northern neighbour, Papua New Guinea. While some of the farms rely solely on commercial trading, others have developed their tourist potential. In fact, the Broome Crocodile Farm in Western Australia has expanded into crocodile breeding from being a fauna park. It already attracts over 30,000 visitors each year.

IN AFRICA

In Africa, Zimbabwe has been at the forefront of crocodile farming, since starting a ranching programme at Lake Kariba back in 1965. Initially, this operated on the basis of hatchlings caught in the wild, but after 500 had been obtained during the first four years of the venture, it became clear that there were several major drawbacks to this approach. Apart from the time taken to obtain them, it was obvious that the hatchlings did not settle immediately into the confines of the ranch, and this could affect their growth rate.

It was therefore decided to rely instead on eggs. Prescribed collecting areas are now laid down, so that there is no risk of damaging the population by taking too many eggs from one locality. Collection is usually carried out during the first week or so of November, about two months after the eggs are laid. This has been shown to be the best time to disturb the eggs, which are located by a probe, without affecting their hatchability.

The young crocodiles emerge about the end of the year. The results show that hatchability of collected eggs is now over 88 per cent, compared with just under 74 per cent in the early 1970s, because of improved management techniques. It has been a feature of the scheme from its inception that a percentage of the offspring must be returned to the wild if the government so requires. This has not proved generally necessary, however, because the crocodile population in Zimbabwe has grown substantially during recent years to around 50,000 individuals, from having been on the verge of extinction in the early 1960s. But around 1000 have been used for restocking and collection permits still state that 5 hatchlings per 100 eggs may ultimately be required for this purpose.

Farming, as distinct from ranching, of crocodiles in Zimbabwe began at the end of the 1970s. At the start, just two farms were involved, and nearly 2000 eggs were laid by their resident population of 87 females. The total continues to grow, however, with hatchability on a par with that of eggs collected in the wild.

A number of neighbouring African states have followed Zimbabwe's example. The key to the success of such enterprises, however, is to ensure that the skin trade cannot provide a conduit for illegally taken hides. Under CITES supervision therefore, special tags have been produced to mark the individual skins. The tag is specially designed so that, once it has been used, there is no possibility that it can be transferred subsequently to another skin.

The tags are individually numbered in sequence and consist of two components, which are kept separate until they are issued. The positioning of the tag on the skin is also laid down by regulations, and this is varied as an additional security measure. The system seems to work effectively and is reasonably straightforward to administer, and Zimbabwe's wild crocodile population continues to thrive.

IN EUROPE

Not all crocodilian farming ventures are successful, however, as demonstrated by Italian attempts to ranch the common caiman. Hatchlings were shipped to Rome from Colombia during the winter, before being moved south. The majority died from the effects of this road journey, and it appears that the methods of husbandry were so unsatisfactory that the survivors did not live long after their arrival. Aside from this sorry episode in the 1970s, there have been no other ventures into large-scale crocodilian ranching in Europe.

IN THE AMERICAS

Across the Atlantic in the USA, Louisiana has become the centre for alligator farming. The studies carried out at the Rockefeller Wildlife Refuge into the farming of these reptiles have provided results which have been of value to workers in other countries as well.

At the present time, research is being directed towards identifying the optimum conditions for growth. It even appears that the alligators respond well to local Cajun music, which helps to reduce external stresses on them, such as during the cleaning of pens in their vicinity. Other data obtained here has revealed that captive-bred alligators nest at an earlier age than wild stock and, ultimately, prove more prolific.

There are presently 13 alligator farms in Louisiana, holding over 20,000 individuals. The emphasis is placed on the provision of controlled-environment housing for optimal growth rates. This is economically feasible, although larger alligators above the minimum size required by the skin trade are still taken from the wild.

No conflict exists between farming and wild quotas, therefore, as they are supplying different skins for the market. Stock from Louisiana was sent to El Salvador during the late 1960s as part of an early experiment to discover whether the alligators would grow more quickly in a warm climate without the necessity for periods of aestivation, and this appears to have been the case.

About the same time, the Cuban government also ventured into crocodile farming, but allowed hybridization between the two indigenous species – the American crocodile and the Cuban crocodile (*Crocodylus rhombifer*). The original purpose behind the project had been to conserve the latter species, since its habitat was being utilized increasingly for the production of sugar cane. Cropping of surplus stock for skins was a longer-term aim.

In Mexico, attempts have been made to farm Morelet's crocodile (*Crocodylus moreletii*), with funding originating from the World Wide Fund for Nature (WWF) at the outset. This species is particularly in demand for the leather trade, as it has no osteoderms present on its belly skin, and it has been heavily hunted as a result.

CAUSE FOR CONCERN

Other countries in Central and South America have also contemplated

51

ranching of crocodilians, and some projects are under way. Much still remains to be achieved in this area, especially bearing in mind the vast numbers of common caiman (*Caiman crocodilus*) skins which are still entering international trade. Like the broad-snouted caiman (*Caiman latirostris*) and the black caiman (*Melanosuchus niger*) before it, this species will inevitably decline through its range, especially while poaching remains widespread.

The common caiman has become the last resort of the hunter. Having driven crocodiles and the American alligator, with their larger and more valuable skins, to the verge of extinction, and then the other caimans, there is really no other species left. In order to overcome the problem of osteoderms pitting the leather, the hunters only take strips of skin running from the throat of the caiman down either side of its body, covering the area here from the back to the scales of the belly. Each *chaleco*, as these cuts are called, is then divided to produce two flank skins.

Advances in tanning technology mean that the skins of caimans are now much easier to process, and South America has gained the unenviable reputation for being the world's leading centre for the illicit skin trade. Although protective legislation exists in many countries, it is rarely enforced effectively, and trade has continued largely unchecked. This is a cause for considerable concern amongst those who have battled hard to ensure the future of crocodilians on other continents.

Chapter 3

Form and Function

ANATOMICAL FEATURES

The crocodilian is ideally adapted to its life as a predator. When it is submerged in the water, very little of its body is exposed, apart from its eyes. These are positioned close together, in such a manner that binocular vision is possible. This enables the crocodilian to judge precisely where prey is positioned and to strike with great accuracy.

As crocodilians hunt at night, their eyes have the typical vertical slit-like pupil associated with other nocturnal reptiles, such as the Tokay gecko (*Gekko gecko*). The advantage of this arrangement is that it permits more light to enter the eye and register on the retina than would be possible with a round pupil. As in other night-hunters, there is an additional layer of cells at the back of the retina itself, forming the so-called tapetum lucidum.

This reflective layer directs light passing through the eye back to the retina and so improves the image. It is for this reason that the eyes of crocodilians appear to glow in the dark when a flashlight is shone at

Plate 24   The top of an alligator's skull. Note the relatively high position of the eye sockets and of the nostrils on top of the skull. The brain itself is well protected beneath the heavy bony casing.

Plate 25 Crocodilians have good vision, even when it is quite dark. Note the slit-like rather than round shape of the pupil. The iris itself is generally of a brownish shade, being somewhat lighter in some species than others.

Plate 26 Although it looks dangerous, this Indian wrestler will be able to keep the alligator's mouth closed with virtually no effort.

Plate 27   The musculature for opening the jaws is extremely weak in all
crocodilians, whereas they can shut their jaws with devastating force. It has been
calculated that a crocodilian weighing one tonne could produce a force of 13
tonnes at this stage.

them. With a mixture of both rods and cones forming the retina, crocodilians possess colour vision.

When hunting under water, the eyes of crocodiles are protected by
the transparent nictitating membranes, but clear vision may be difficult in muddy water. Their keen sense of smell then comes into play.
The importance of this sense is reflected by the relatively large area of
the brain which is devoted to olfactory stimuli.

Crocodilians also have acute hearing, with their ears being covered
by tissue flaps high on the head, just below the roof of the cranium. The
flaps serve to shield the openings when the reptile is below water. The
inner ear is highly developed and the auditory canal extends across the
head, presumably to assist in the detection of the presence of prey.
Crocodilians also appear to be sensitive to a wide frequency range, thus
ensuring that their hearing is sufficiently acute to hear their young
calling from within their eggshells.

The brain itself is located relatively high in the cranial cavity, where
it can be warmed readily and is also well protected. Although small in

size, the crocodilian's brain is well adapted, particularly for sensory input. In addition to their senses already mentioned, the scales along the sides of the jaws have pits containing sensory nerve fibres. These undoubtedly assist with the capture of prey, in conjunction with, for example, the sense of smell.

Perhaps strangely, crocodilians lack Jacobsen's organ, an important feature in other reptilian groups, which is used to detect scent molecules in the mouth and connects almost directly to the brain. It has been suggested that, during the embryonic stages of development, evidence of this vomero-nasal organ can be detected.

The absence of Jacobsen's organ may give a clue to the ancestry of today's crocodilians, especially when linked with the well developed olfactory tissue. This pattern is usually linked with terrestrial rather than aquatic reptiles and so it seems plausible that crocodilians are descended from essentially land-dwelling stock, and have later returned, at least partially, to water.

Having detected suitable prey, crocodilians can snap their jaws shut with considerable force. Based on research carried out in France, it has been calculated that a large crocodile can exert a crushing force equivalent to 13 tonnes. Alligators are reputed to be able to smash the leg of

Plate 28   The fearsome array of teeth in the jaws of a crocodilian are being replaced throughout the animal's life, and clear signs of wear are apparent on some of the teeth here.

a cow without difficulty, and can easily crush the shells of turtles in their jaws, but, strangely, the musculature responsible for the opening of the jaws is surprisingly weak.

This fact has been skilfully exploited by the Seminole Indians in North America in their performances of alligator wrestling. In fact, it is very easy to keep the mouth of a large crocodilian closed. Indeed, with a crocodilian up to 2 m ($6\frac{1}{2}$ ft) in length, a rubber band can be relied upon for this task.

The teeth of crocodilians are potentially lethal, however, and the force of the jaws when they close will drive the teeth well into their victim's flesh. Teeth tend to be conical in shape, with sharp points, and are anchored in their sockets by means of connective tissue.

Unlike the teeth of mammals, crocodilians' teeth are replaced throughout life, although the process becomes slower as they grow older. Teeth are shed alternatively along the jaw, to minimize the impact of replacement. Interestingly, in young crocodilians, the teeth towards the back of the mouth are replaced first, whereas in adults, the direction of replacement is reversed.

The new teeth develop in a separate pocket, located towards the

Plate 29   The teeth are constantly growing and being shed throughout the crocodilian's life and, although this may appear to be a random process, it is arranged so that at no stage will an individual be unable to catch prey effectively. In very old animals, however, lost teeth may not be replaced.

Plate 30   A crocodile's teeth are well suited not for chewing but rather for inflicting maximum injury on prey and retaining a firm grip. There is no risk of them chewing their way out of their enclosure.

midline of the body rather than on the outer side of existing teeth. Each one subsequently moves to occupy the conical hollow at the base of the corresponding tooth. Here it will grow, finally displacing its predecessor. The old root breaks down, and the crown is shed. By the time that it has reached a length of 3.9 m ($12\frac{3}{4}$ ft), a Nile crocodile may already have used 45 sets of teeth! In old crocodilians, it appears that teeth are shed without being replaced, and this causes wider gaps than normal to appear between the teeth in the jaws.

The tongue within the mouth is broad and attached to the bottom of the mouth. It has no role in restraining prey, a function undertaken by the jaws alone. At the tip of the snout, the teeth actually interlock, clasping any animal with deadly effect. Those in the jaws of narrow-snouted crocodilians, such as the gharials, are particularly sharp. In the case of small prey, such as a fish, careful manipulation from the front of the mouth to the back sees it first impaled, and then swallowed into the buccal cavity by a deft movement of the crocodilian's head in an upward direction.

Larger prey presents more of a challenge, especially if the animal concerned attempts to break free. The neck of the crocodilian is therefore given greater support by the presence of overlapping processes on the cervical (neck) vertebrae. The crocodilian can effectively resist the response of a much bigger creature, such as a buffalo, and drag it off

Plate 31   The tongue of the crocodilian is essentially immobile, being fixed to the floor of the mouth.

Plate 32   The jaws of aquatic crocodiles, which feed mainly on fish, are surprisingly narrow, but contain devastating rows of teeth, as shown by this African slender-snouted crocodile (*Crocodylus cataphractus*).

Plate 33   Larger mammals are taken by other species, including the notorious Indo-Pacific crocodile (*Crocodylus porosus*). Wallabies feature amongst the prey of this species in Australia.

into deeper water, where its demise will be inevitable. Crocodilians will seek to drown their prey, and then roll it in such a way that chunks of flesh can be pulled off and swallowed whole.

THE FEEDING PROCESS
Even as a young hatchling, the crocodilian possesses the basic instincts to prove an effective hunter. Moving quietly, and remaining hidden for as long as possible before striking out, youngsters take a variety of prey, ranging from insects to amphibians and fish.

DIET AND DIGESTION
It is clear from studies carried out involving the Nile crocodile, that the diet alters considerably as the animals grow older and larger. Insects

are a vital food source for hatchlings up to 50 cm (20 in) long, with fish, birds and mammals featuring in the case of small adults, between 2.5 m and 3 m (8–10 ft) in length. By the time that the Nile crocodile has grown to a maximum of about 5 m (16 ft), mammals form the major part of its diet, followed by reptiles. A degree of cannibalism is certainly not unknown, but bearing in mind that over 30 per cent of the crocodiles studied had empty stomachs, it is clear that they do not feed every day, as had previously been thought. It seems unlikely that the Nile crocodile actually kills more than 50 times annually on this basis.

Food can be stored in the gullet, if the stomach is already full. The stomach is comprised of three chambers. The main area, the thick-walled fundus, with its muscular component, is often compared to the gizzard of a bird. In front of this is the cardiac region, which is relatively smooth, in contrast to the fundus where rugae cover the surface. The rear pyloric section contains glandular material, liberating gastrin and other enzymes. Perhaps the most unusual feature of the crocodilian's digestive system is the presence of gastroliths within its stomach. These are stones which the reptile has deliberately swallowed, rather like a granivorous bird searching for grit. Studies have shown that hatchling crocodilians under one year old do not have any gastroliths.

Interestingly, in older individuals, the gastroliths account for a relatively standard 1 per cent of body weight. Even in areas where stones are scarce, crocodilians will seek them out, perhaps travelling miles for this purpose. They will also swallow pieces of pottery and glass if these are more readily available.

One of the earliest explanations for the crocodilian's desire for pebbles was put forward during 1766 by the scientific explorer F. Hasselquist. He believed that the stones were used to grind up the food within the crocodilian's stomach. The presence of gastroliths is not associated just with contemporary crocodilians. They have also been found in association with the fossilized remains of their predecessors.

It is, however, surprising that young crocodilians, feeding on hard-shelled invertebrates during their first months of life, apparently have no need for gastroliths. Hugh Cott, famous for his work on the Nile crocodile, proposed an alternative explanation, suggesting that such stones were required for buoyancy in adults. They would shift the centre of gravity within the crocodilian's body, so that it could float easily, while, at the same time, acting as ballast when the crocodile attempted to drag heavy prey into water.

Evidence to support this theory comes from the movements of hatchlings in deep water. Initially, they are unable to float flat at the surface, in contrast to an adult with gastroliths present. They tend to lie at an unusual angle, which is corrected later in life.

Investigation into the role of gastroliths was carried out by workers at the Yale Peabody Museum in the USA, during 1968. A dead mouse was injected with a radio-opaque material and fed to a caiman, and the passage of the rodent through the digestive tract was monitored and recorded on videotape.

Suddenly, after a period of 36 hours, the gastroliths in the stomach became active, apparently crushing the mouse and liberating the radio-opaque material. Therefore, it appears that gastroliths are involved in the digestive process, but this does not mean that they have no role in ensuring the buoyancy of the crocodilian in the water as well.

As a result of these reptiles' desire for gastroliths, researchers have been able to persuade them to swallow radio-tracking devices. On occasions, oddities such as bullets may be found alongside gastroliths in the stomach. In such cases, it is likely that the crocodilian seized an animal which had previously been shot and, although its body was effectively digested, the bullet remained intact in the stomach.

Crocodilians have a very efficient digestive system, which is quite capable of dissolving bone. Chitin, however, which form the hard body casing of many invertebrates, can, like turtle shell and hair, only be digested slowly. Indeed, solid mats of hair are sometimes recovered from the otherwise empty stomachs of crocodilians.

Their digestive juices are exceedingly acid, with a pH value as low as 2. It takes at least a day or so for a meal to be broken down, depending on the environmental temperature. Absorption of nutrients, as in mammals, occurs during passage through the small intestine.

Most of the nutritional value of the food, in energy terms, is stored within the crocodilian's body as fat. Storage areas include the tail and back, as well as the mesenteric organs of the abdomen. As a result, crocodilians are well adapted to survive for many months without feeding, relying on their stores of body fat to sustain them.

There may be a considerable difference therefore in the weights of individuals of similar sizes, depending on their feeding habits. As an example, in the case of the American alligator, a 3.5 m (11.5 ft) individual tipped the scales at 268 kg (591 lb), while a larger specimen, 3.7 m (12 ft) long weighed in at just 209 kg (460 lb), yet both appeared healthy.

A mature crocodilian may be able to live for as long as two years in the absence of suitable prey. It is possible that this ability may have assisted the group to survive the extinction of the dinosaurs, when there were clearly dramatic changes taking place on the planet.

The effect of this fat storage on metabolism is one of contrasts. For most of its life, the crocodilian is relatively sluggish but periods of major exertion occur when it is feeding. Then it will switch to anaerobic

Plate 34   Crocodilians often remain largely hidden, resembling, for example, logs in the water. They can move very close to the shore and then seize prey as it comes to drink.

Plate 35   The lunge of this American crocodile (*Crocodylus acutus*) shows the speed at which a crocodile can strike. In some cases, they may venture a short distance out of water in order to make a kill.

metabolism to sustain its activity, and the concentration of lactic acid in its blood rises rapidly to levels which would prove fatal in other species.

Under normal circumstances, once the prey has been caught and overpowered, the lactic acid levels will fall in the presence of oxygen. But it is now realised that, physiologically, a prolonged struggle can be

63

dangerous, especially to a big crocodilian. The concentration of lactic acid in the blood will continue to rise under such circumstances, and death from acidosis may become inevitable after such a major period of exertion. This is the likely reason for the death of large crocodiles, such as Sweetheart (see page 25) shortly after capture. They die, in effect, from over-exertion.

Because of the reliance on fat metabolism, the growth rate of young wild crocodiles is slow. This fact has been dramatically demonstrated by comparing the development of wild crocodilians with that of those reared on farms where a constant supply of food is available in a controlled environment. Hibernation for example, which occurs in the American alligator in the colder months, results in a reduced food intake and slow growth rate.

HUNTING STRATEGIES

There is a marked difference in the feeding habits of the various species, depending to some extent on the shape of their snouts. Those with narrow snouts, such as the gharial (*Gavialis gangeticus*) and the African slender-snouted crocodile (*Crocodylus cataphractus*), will feed mainly on fish, although they also take other aquatic creatures such as crabs, as well as birds and small mammals. The reduction in snout width affords them greater mobility under water, although they are unable to take larger prey out of the water.

The heavier-snouted crocodiles are able to subdue a much wider range of animals, and prey to a greater extent on mammals. The Indo-Pacific crocodile, for example, will take farmstock, including cattle and horses, and other creatures of similar size. The Nile crocodile is another member of this group, known to prey on people, as well as animals such as zebra and buffalo.

Such crocodilians are opportunistic predators and hunt by ambushing their prey. They remain concealed in the water, silently approaching close enough to their intended victim to launch a devastating strike. A crocodile can run a short distance up the bank at considerable speed to grab hold of its target. If drinking, the unfortunate animal is likely to be seized by its head, and dragged into the water where it can be drowned. Birds are also at risk of being taken in a similar fashion, even if they attempt to fly off, since crocodiles can leap out of the water almost vertically.

Although it has long been stated that crocodilians also use their powerful tails to knock potential prey off balance, there appears to be little real evidence to support this view. They have, however, been observed using their heads to smash against the legs of larger animals, giving them a better opportunity to seize their prey while it is off balance. Nevertheless, crocodilians are patient hunters and will wait for a considerable period of time in an area where the opportunity for making a kill is good.

Specialist hunting strategies have been evolved in some instances, as in the case of the fish-eating African slender-snouted crocodile. It will swim close to a river bank, with its tail curved in the direction of the shore, driving small schools of fish ahead of it into the shallows. These can then be trawled up, as it sweeps the area between the bank and its body using its slender jaws. Fish are always swallowed head first, to minimize the risk of any spines sticking into the crocodilian's throat. Sometimes, large fish are broken down into pieces by a fierce shaking of the head from side to side, or they may be taken on to land.

In South America, the common caiman (*Caiman crocodilus*) will prey on a variety of fish, including the notorious piranha (*Serrasalmus piraya*). President Theodore Roosevelt witnessed a remarkable clash of these two predatory creatures. A caiman which had been shot was afterwards viciously attacked by the piranhas which scented its blood. It rushed out of the water, showing the teeth marks of the fish clearly on its body.

There is growing evidence that crocodilians, at least of some species,

Plate 36   The hind feet are clearly webbed, reflecting the crocodilian's lifestyle, which is inevitably dependent on water. Some species are more aquatic than others and these tend to be the most streamlined in shape.

do hunt collectively. At Lake St Lucia, in Natal, the annual mullet migration attracts a large number of crocodiles. They combine effectively to block the path of the fish, at a spot called the Narrows, which is barely 500 m (550 yd) across. Each crocodile takes the fish as they move within range. There is no fighting over positioning, and none breaks rank, which would allow the mullet to escape.

When there is a large kill, such as a buffalo, it is not unusual for a group of crocodilians to converge on the carcass. This actually benefits the individual responsible, since otherwise, it would almost certainly have difficulty in dismembering the prey by itself. Its teeth are not sufficiently adept to chew the carcass into pieces. Instead, the crocodilian will grasp a limb, and then spin in the water, ripping the limb from the body. This process is made much easier when other crocodilians hold the prey steady. Each feeds in turn, without apparent conflict.

The stomach of a crocodilian is surprisingly small and, inevitably, it would not be able to swallow the whole of a large herbivore. Having eaten their fill, the crocodilians will return later to a carcass, but there is no real evidence to show that they attempt to hide the remains under the water or in any specific locality. Crocodiles will scavenge, but generally prefer freshly killed food, so the concept of a 'larder' where a carcass is kept is rather misleading.

MOBILITY

Crocodilians are well adapted for an aquatic environment. Their webbed feet may be of some assistance when swimming, but the main thrust comes from their powerful tail. This is moved from side to side, in a rippling 'S'-shaped pattern, which is quite obvious when the reptile is resting at the surface. They prefer relatively calm areas of water, where they can breathe without difficulty through the nostrils which are located at the far end of the snout forming the nasal disc on the top of the head. In choppy waters, they are forced to raise the snout to a more vertical position, and this reduces their swimming capabilities.

The front feet in particular are usually held close to the body while the crocodilian is in the water. Moving on land, crocodiles frequently appear cumbersome, especially when they are moving slowly, in the so-called 'high walking' style. The tail is then dragged along behind the body, but once they start to run it is moved from side to side.

When moving quickly over short distances, to catch prey for example, and galloping out of the water, crocodilians can move at speeds equivalent to 18 kph (11 mph), although they will cover less than 100 m (109 yd) in this fashion. Johnston's crocodile is a species which regularly gallops, whereas the Indo-Pacific crocodile rarely moves in this fashion, possibly because of its greater bulk. Small crocodilians are generally more adept on land than their larger relatives.

As a result of their metabolism, crocodilians usually prefer to avoid covering large distances overland, although they can do so when necessary. Loss of habitat, caused by the drying up of rivers, can evoke this response.

BREATHING

It is not possible for a crocodilian to close its mouth properly when it is submerged, since it has no lips. As a result, it cannot exclude water from its mouth. Under normal circumstances, when its face was beneath water, it would be prevented from breathing through the nostrils on the top of the snout. Water would flow down the trachea into the lungs, causing the animal to drown. But in the present-day crocodilian, this difficulty has been overcome by the extension of the palatine, maxillary and pterygoid bones into the roof of the mouth, which creates the secondary palate.

Air is drawn over this bone down to the rear of the mouth, where it enters the pharynx, and so reaches the trachea. Water is excluded rostrally in front of this region by a combination of the glottis with the basihyal valve. Then, when the crocodilian actually submerges, muscles act to seal the external nostrils located in the nasal plate.

Crocodilians have evolved a primitive diaphragm, which is in the

Plate 37   The crocodilian's nostrils are located at the end of the snout, on its dorsal surface. This enables the reptile to breathe without difficulty while remaining almost totally submerged out of sight.

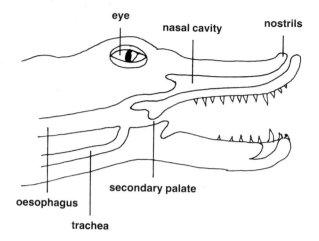

Fig. 1   The breathing system of a crocodilian, showing the positioning and significance of the secondary palate.

form of connective tissue attached to the liver, linked by muscles to the pelvic bones. When the crocodilian breathes out, the liver effectively moves forward under muscular control. On inspiration, the situation is reversed and the liver shifts posteriorly. Once submerged, water pressure causes expiration, with little if any muscular involvement, but inspiration then requires increased effort from the muscles. The movement of the liver back and forth in this fashion is sometimes described as the 'hepatic piston'.

Studies with the Indo-Pacific crocodile suggest that it rarely stays submerged for much longer than $6\frac{1}{2}$ minutes under normal circumstances, before returning to the surface to replenish its oxygen supply. There could well be differences between various species, however, in terms of their abilities to withstand an oxygen debt caused by long-term submersion.

In a rather gruesome series of experiments conducted during 1925, it was noted that young caimans drowned quite rapidly, within 34–72 minutes after being immersed in water. American alligators, however, withstood this situation for considerably longer, surviving for a minimum of 320 minutes and up to 365 minutes.

THERMO-REGULATION

Oxygen requirements are of course temperature-dependent to some extent, notably in the case of reptiles, which are poikilothermic and popularly but rather erroneously described as 'cold-blooded'. Crocodilians are no exception and rely on their environment to provide their body warmth. The rate of heat loss is influenced by body size, with larger crocodilians having greater control over thermo-regulation than hatchlings. These are much more susceptible to chilling than adults, because they have a bigger surface area to volume ratio. As a consequence, they can cool down more quickly, but conversely, will gain warmth more rapidly from their surroundings as well.

Remaining close to water assists a crocodilian in maintaining its body temperature within optimum limits. Water temperatures show less extremes of variation than air temperature. By altering its pattern of behaviour through the day, the crocodilian can ensure as far as possible that it is not subject to extremes of thermal stress.

In the morning, for example, American alligators will come on to land, basking to gain the benefit of the sun's rays. Then, as midday approaches and the sun becomes stronger, the reptiles will tend to retreat back to the water, to prevent overheating. They will then start to bask again in the late afternoon, before returning to the sanctuary of the water overnight. This pattern may be influenced by a circadian rhythm, although it appears to be largely temperature-dependent. On a cold day for example, when there is considerable cloud cover, crocodilians will remain in the water for longer periods than normal.

The circulatory system plays a vital part in thermo-regulation, because by alterations in the blood flow to the extremities, heat can be conserved or lost from the body. At the centre of this system is the heart, which, in contrast to that of all other reptiles, has four distinct chambers, resembling the mammalian arrangement. The partition in the ventricle ensures that oxygenated and deoxygenated blood are kept separate, although slight mixing is possible via the foramen of Panizza, just outside the ventricles.

When the crocodilian submerges, however, this foramen (unique to crocodilians) closes, ensuring that blood containing oxygen is directed to the brain and heart itself, whereas other body organs receive a deoxygenated supply for this period. Changes in heart rate, coupled with alterations in the diameter of blood vessels ensure that crocodilians can either shunt their blood into superficial vessels, or, as when diving, reduce this flow and conserve body heat accordingly.

Two species of crocodilian, the American alligator and the Chinese alligator, occur in latitudes where the temperature can fall below freezing during the winter. Both species excavate burrows into which they can retreat. Those of the American alligator are up to 1.5 m (5 ft) in length. These are connected with longer passages, which can be dug out over a number of years, reaching lengths of 18 m (60 ft). The

Plate 38   Basking is an important part of the crocodilian's lifestyle, enabling it to raise its body temperature under the sun's rays when the water is relatively cool. The significance of gaping is probably also linked with thermo-regulation. The crocodile may be able to cool its head, while the rest of its body warms up.

alligators use their feet to scrape away the mud and vegetation, occasionally resorting to their teeth to overcome a stubborn root obstructing their path.

In Florida 'gator holes' are a conspicuous part of the local landscape. They usually contain water, even at the driest times of year, and can provide an important refuge for young alligators and other wildlife. The alligators dig out the bottom of these basins so that they can retreat into deeper water than would otherwise be possible. It seems that this technique arose more because of the threat of drought than cold.

Basins of this type are conspicuous because there is no vegetation growing at their centres. In contrast, actual dens are harder to observe. Through the northern part of their range, alligators remain in their dens from about October through to March. They will emerge, however, on days when the weather is warm, basking in the sunshine. Although often filled with water along some of their length, the dens usually incorporate holes where the alligator can breathe directly from the air above.

Alligators in water are potentially at risk from being trapped beneath ice, where they would be unable to breathe. They respond by keeping the tip of their snout exposed, with the rest of their head and body submerged. This so-called 'icing response' means that, although they may subsequently be frozen into the ice, provided that their nostrils remain clear, they can survive quite adequately in such conditions, awaiting a thaw. Their internal body temperature may plummet at this stage to just 5°C (41°F), compared with a normal figure of around 33°C (91°F).

Other species found in tropical areas will burrow to survive the effects of drought. Nile crocodiles respond in this way, although hatchlings are said to use their mouths rather than their fore feet for this task, which is frequently carried out at night. Burrows, extending for 10 m (33 ft) or more, may be used communally. Up to 15 crocodiles have been recorded in a single chamber of this type, close to the Songwe River in Tanzania.

Burrowing behaviour has also been noted in India, where the mugger will bury into mud to escape the searing heat during the dry season. The American crocodile acts in a similar fashion to the alligator in the Zapata Swampland in the southwest of Cuba, although here again the enemy is drought rather than cold.

SOCIAL INTERACTIONS

Where areas of water are drying up, and crocodilians are forced to live

Plate 39   Alligators show a distinct daily routine in terms of basking behaviour when the weather is good. They may return to water if disturbed, however, and usually spend the night here as well.

in closer contact than normal, it is usual to find a variety of age groups represented and living together in virtual harmony. Conflicts under these circumstances are rare, even when the reptiles are grossly over-crowded. A study of one such water hole in Venezuela, which was just 50 m (165 ft) across, and a maximum of 2 m (6 ft) deep, revealed that it was accommodating no less than 200 common caimans. Although some bigger males were clearly dominant, there was no overt fighting.

Dominance is an essential part of crocodilian communities, with the larger and more aggressive animals in a group occupying the top of the hierarchy. Actual physical conflicts are rarely seen, however, since the weaker individual usually backs off by submerging and swimming away. If fighting does occur, the dominant male will seek to bite his opponent around the base of the tail, close to the hind legs. But even if an individual is wounded, and possibly loses the tip of its tail, it is likely to recover. In this instance, the tip regenerates as cartilage. Clearly there are very effective protective mechanisms within the crocodilian's blood which guard against infection and resulting tissue necrosis.

Territories of males vary quite widely in extent, depending partly on the species concerned. On crocodile farms, in order to minimize terri-torial aggression, the area of water often takes the form of channels, rather than a central pond which might be monopolized by a single male. Crocodilians can prove quite sociable in these surroundings. It

Plate 40   Crocodilians vary in their acceptance of others of their species. They are generally more tolerant outside the breeding season, and when the water level is low.

appears clear that they will sometimes seek the company of others of their species, lying on top of each other.

Outbreaks of territorial aggression are most likely to arise during the breeding period. At this stage, even female alligators will become territorial, driving off others which threaten to encroach on their established domain. This can spill over into physical assaults and may even result in the death of the newcomer.

COMMUNICATION

Crocodilians possess four scent glands which produce a musky odour. One pair is located along the lower jaw and may be visible when the crocodilian's mouth is open. The second pair is found within the cloaca, but their precise role is unclear. It appears that they may assist individuals to recognize each other. Alligators' hatchlings will certainly respond to the scent of an adult male.

Another means of communication is provided by vocalization, which is a feature unique to crocodilians, out of all reptiles. The American alligator is the most vocal species, possibly because of its habitat, where visual contact may be hard to maintain. It is even possible to distinguish individual alligators on the basis of their calls. Bellowing becomes more common at the start of the breeding season, but may also be triggered by significant changes in the weather, such as a violent thunderstorm.

The call itself is best described as resembling the roar of a lion, with that of females having a higher pitch. Hatchlings tend to bark or grunt, and their calls can attract adults in the area. Mimicry of the young alligator's call used to be a means adopted by hunters to lure large individuals within range.

The bellow of an alligator is audible over a considerable distance, at least 150 m (165 yd) and, in response, all others in the area may start calling back. The notes may also be picked up under water. It appears that vocalization is of considerable importance when there are young hatchlings and may serve to maintain the integrity of a group.

Other methods of crocodilian communication utilize the aquatic environment directly. The most widely recognized of these is head-slapping. The crocodilian rests with its lower jaw on the surface of the water and slaps its upper jaw down, causing a loud pop as the jaws meet and then a splash. It may be a sign of dominance in a given area and certainly commands attention. Such activity may be followed by bubbles of air being exhaled from the nostrils. This appears to be an actual means of communication in a number of species.

Thrashing the tail, especially in water, also reverberates over a wide area. A more subtle but nevertheless significant use of water for communication purposes is the production of so-called 'infra-sound'. As the word suggests, this is barely audible but, with the crocodilian lying just below the surface of the water and twitching its body, the reverberating waves spread out over a considerable distance. In the case of the American alligator, this can form a prelude to roaring.

The gharial has a slightly different approach to communication in the water, since it has never been observed to engage in head-slapping. Instead, during the breeding period, it claps its jaws under water. The blowing of bubbles also appears to be a significant courtship preliminary of this species.

SURVIVAL IN SALT WATER

The majority of crocodilians today are found in areas of fresh water, but both the American and Indo-Pacific species, as well as the common caiman, can also be encountered in salty environments. On occasions, the Indo-Pacific crocodile may even be found a considerable distance

Plate 41   The Indo-Pacific crocodile is not infrequently encountered throughout its range in tropical seas, and this has helped it to colonize many island locations between Asia and Australia.

out to sea, well away from river estuaries, and hatchlings have also been reared successfully in sea water.

As a protection against becoming overloaded with salt, this species has prominent glands at the back of the tongue which secrete a concentrated sodium chloride solution. The thick skin of this crocodile helps to prevent loss of fluid by osmosis in a marine environment, which would lead to rapid dehydration and death.

Interestingly, salt glands are present in all crocodiles but not in alligators and caimans. It has been suggested that the crocodiles may be descended from a marine ancestor, but, it is more likely that, although these glands have become very efficient in the Indo-Pacific crocodile, their prime function was to counter the build-up of salts following prolonged dehydration.

Crocodilian kidneys are not adapted to deal with sodium chloride. Certainly in the American crocodile, this task is undertaken in the cloaca. Under normal circumstances, this salt is absorbed well here, although the level of absorption is lower following dehydration.

SKIN

Another feature of both the crocodiles best adapted for life in salt water is the great reduction of the protective covering of so-called armour

Plate 42   Fighting between individuals does occur on occasions. Cannibalism is most likely to take place when there are many juveniles in an area, especially if they are of different sizes.

over the neck. The body casing of crocodilians is made up of scales, which vary in shape and strength. As they grow, crocodilians do not shed their whole body casing in the same way as snakes, but instead lose individual scutes, which are replaced. Along the back, there are bony deposits within the individual scales, which are called osteoderms. Apart from providing increased protection, these particular scutes also have a complex blood supply. This enables heat transference to take place readily when the crocodilian is basking.

The extent of the osteoderms varies according to both the species and the individual populations. It is of particular significance to the leather trade, because osteoderms impart a rougher texture to the finished skin, and colour slightly differently. The Indo-Pacific crocodile, with its smooth belly free from osteoderms, has been one of the most popular species in the trade. In contrast, caimans in general are well protected by osteoderms and, until quite recently, have tended to be overlooked by the trade as a result.

The heavy body armour on the back is also important, not only physiologically, but also practically, since it serves to protect the internal organs as well. The tail never contains osteoderms, although the scutes here are both thickened and vascularized. The double row of scutes along the tail may improve the crocodilian's swimming ability, but it is not unusual for part of the tail to be lost through encounters with other crocodilians. This can be regenerated to a limited extent.

PREDATION AND MORTALITY

There are few animals which will prey on mature crocodilians, although cannibalism amongst sub-adults is not unknown. The extent of this behaviour is hard to assess, however, but it appears more prevalent in some populations than others. Adults are generally protective towards hatchlings and it would seem that cannibalism is most likely to occur between juveniles of different sizes. This may be a survival instinct in an area where food is in short supply or where overcrowding is likely to occur.

In the case of the Indo-Pacific crocodile, where the population has been heavily hunted in the past, it has been noted that the number of hatchlings grew rapidly in the early stages after hunting was banned. Subsequently, it was observed that the older offspring were preying on younger hatchlings, which curbed the population growth. Crocodiles are long-lived animals, so that the total loss of hatchlings in some years would not necessarily affect the overall status of the population, either immediately or over the longer term.

Deaths resulting from fighting during the breeding period are not unknown, but again, relatively little information about this area of crocodilian behaviour has been recorded. Some male Nile crocodiles will certainly fight to the death, and usually the younger, smaller individual in such an encounter is the casualty. Having chosen a nesting area, females also may occasionally battle to defend their territory from a rival, and this can also result in the death of the newcomer.

By the time that a crocodilian has grown to a length of 1 m (3 ft), there are few predators which will risk an encounter with it. Big cats may occasionally prey on crocodilians, however, especially the jaguar (*Panthera onca*), which ranges from the southern part of the USA down into South America as far as northern Argentina. They may strike at nesting caimans and, according to one report from Theodore Roosevelt's expedition to Brazil, they can even penetrate the reptile's armour at the neck with their teeth, once they have jumped down on to its back. The jaguar then rips open the relatively soft belly of the crocodilian, once it has been rendered immobile. Lions were seen to kill a Nile crocodile on one occasion when the reptile tried to steal their kill, but such encounters, like those with tigers and leopards, are rare.

Large snakes, notably the giant anaconda (*Eunectes murinus*) can also represent a threat to crocodilians. This particular snake is semi-aquatic by nature and can grow to at least 9 m (30 ft) in length. Thus it is a formidable predator of even large caimans, although these do not appear to form a significant part of its diet.

Aggressive encounters with large mammals can also sometimes spell disaster for crocodilians. In many part of Africa, for example, Nile crocodiles can be found living alongside hippopotamuses. Although a vegetarian by nature, the hippopotamus (*Hippotamus amphibius*) is a very robust animal, and cows are especially belligerent when they have a calf. A Nile crocodile will rarely molest an adult hippopotamus, but it may try to steal a calf, although this carries a not inconsiderable degree of risk. The mother, equipped with fearsome canine teeth in her lower jaw, can crush even a large crocodile, inflicting mortal injuries.

Similarly, on occasions, both elephants and rhinoceroses may attack crocodiles if their offspring are threatened and they are quite capable of killing such reptiles. Battles with elephants can be ferocious encounters. During the 1860s in Natal, a Nile crocodile was observed to seize the hind leg of an elephant at a water hole. The elephant charged out of the water, dragging the crocodile with it, and another member of the herd then killed the crocodile by squashing it under its feet. After this, the injured elephant hurled the carcass into a tree, where it became stuck. Other accounts also describe this peculiar aggressive behaviour, which can leave a dead crocodile perched up to 4.6 m (15 ft) above the ground.

Plate 43   The anaconda (*Eunectes murinus*) is one of the few species to prey throughout its range on even large crocodilians in Central and South America.

Climatic factors rarely play a part in crocodilian mortality, as they are well adapted to survive under adverse conditions. Occasionally, however, adult alligators may die from respiratory complications caused by exposure to freezing conditions, but this is not common.

In contrast, human predation has brought many species of crocodilian to the brink of extinction, although this may not be caused directly by hunting. Investigations into the causes of death in American alligators in Florida between 1971 and 1984 revealed that 19 of the 25 documented cases resulted from human interference. Automobile kills accounted for just over 50 per cent of such deaths, especially on roads which backed directly on to areas of swampland. It has been suggested that, in order to allow alligators to cross safely, such roads should be raised in the future, with culverts provided for the use of alligators.

Changes to existing areas of habitat probably represent the greatest overall threat to many crocodilian populations today. It has been shown in Florida that alterations in water management practices in the vicinity of the Everglades National Park have meant that nest flooding is becoming a serious problem. It has led to a decline in the number of young alligators in the Everglades, while elsewhere in northern Florida, ponds and other areas of habitat are drying up because of lack of water.

Plate 44   Slow-moving crocodilians are at risk from automobiles and this is the major cause of death in some areas.

Plate 45   The presence of osteoderms has been utilized by scientists to investigate the methods of ageing individual crocodilians reliably. A small piece of osteoderm can be removed without causing any long-term damage.

Little reliable data is available on the lifespan of adult crocodilians in the wild, but they may live for over half a century, according to records of zoological collections. Signs of senility, such as lack of teeth, are invariably noticeable in alligators over 50 years old. It seems likely, therefore, that this is about their maximum lifespan.

Indeed, the longest which an American alligator has lived in captivity is 66 years. It was acquired by Adelaide Zoo as a 2-year-old juvenile in 1914, and died there in September 1978. Other crocodilians would appear to have a similar lifespan, although it has been suggested that huge Nile crocodiles, around 5.5 m (18 ft) in length could be about 100 years old. But size is no real indication of a crocodilian's age. Even members of the same species and age may show a considerable difference in growth rate, depending on environmental factors.

Investigations in this field are now relying much more on a study of bone growth and development. Osteoderms can be removed from living crocodilians, typically from the vicinity of the neck, after the animal has been given a sedative and a local anaesthetic. These can then be sectioned, stained and assessed under a microscope. Comparisons of crocodiles of known ages show that assessment is more accurate for younger animals; a 15 per cent error appears for crocodilians around 46 years of age.

Chapter 4

Reproduction

All crocodilians reproduce by means of eggs, and sexual maturity is influenced both by the size and age of the individual. It is usually impossible to distinguish the sexes visually, although it appears that, in all cases, males are significantly larger than females. In young American alligators, the difference in size, which is probably under hormonal control, starts to become apparent once they are three years old.

Sexual maturity is reached once the crocodilians are 1.9 m (6 ft) in overall length and, since males grow more quickly, they are mature by about seven years old. Females are unlikely to lay before they are nine years old, although these figures are influenced by their area of distribution. Maturity occurs later in more northerly regions, where feeding activity is generally lower because of the climate.

COURTSHIP

The courtship process has been well studied in the case of the American alligator. Males start to display soon after their emergence from winter isolation, in April. This activity continues through until May and lasts overall for about two months. The bellowing calls of both males and females are clearly audible at this time and the frequency of head-slapping (see page 73) also increases.

Female alligators generally encourage a response from a male, with pair bonding being preceded by careful contact. This includes touching snouts and gentle nudging around the neck. Preliminary courtship can last for two or three hours, and one partner may break away at this stage, leaving the other on its own, to search for another mate.

Subsequently, each member of the pair will gently submerge the other, before, finally, the male mounts the female. He restrains her by placing his fore legs around her neck, and she may turn slightly on her side, to facilitate penetration. Copulation is usually completed within a few minutes, and there is no further contact between the partners, although, being polygamous, it is possible that they may mate again.

Males remain fertile for about a month during the courtship period, and larger males are able to mate effectively over the longest period. Similarly, the bigger females will mate before smaller, younger individuals, which means that the most mature animals will have the best opportunity to reproduce in any year. It is not unusual, therefore, for the nests of young alligators to contain a relatively high percentage of

Plate 46   Size rather than age is significant in determining sexual maturity in crocodilians. Alligators grow at different rates through their range, and those found in colder northern areas grow more slowly and mature later than their southern counterparts.

infertile eggs and, certainly, not all females breed every year. In Louisiana, only about 60 per cent of mature female alligators will nest annually and, in South Carolina, this figure falls to just 29.5 per cent.

NESTING STRATEGIES

Following mating, it may be a further month before the female is ready to lay her eggs. During this time, she will prepare a nest. The type of nest depends upon the species concerned, although all but one species of crocodilian opt for either a nest mound of earth and vegetation, with the eggs laid at its centre, or a simple hole dug in the ground.

The American crocodile is the exception to this rule, because some of the females will only make a simple hole for their eggs, and not a mound. This behaviour occurs on the coast of Florida, where a small population of these crocodilians is found. They usually nest on the beach, often choosing remote localities in mangrove areas and on small islands in Florida Bay itself.

The nest is dug out at night over a period of several weeks, the site itself being above the high-water mark. The female may also construct

Plate 47   Inhabiting areas of tropical forest can pose particular problems when it comes to the hatching of eggs.

a den for herself nearby, as well as some secondary nest sites, where a few eggs will be laid. Presumably, by laying in several localities, there is a better likelihood that at least some eggs will hatch without being detected by predators.

Elsewhere through its range, particularly where it is more numerous, as on the Dominican Republic in the Caribbean, the American crocodile nests exclusively in this fashion. But, occasionally, in Florida, it resorts to constructing the more typical crocodilian nest. This may be for climatic reasons, as the heat generated within a nest mound containing decaying vegetation is likely to be much greater than if the eggs were simply buried in the ground. The ambient temperature tends to be about 0.5–3°C (0.9–5°F) higher in such surroundings. Could it be that this is a climatic response here at the northern tip of its distribution to ensure better hatchability?

Crocodilians inhabiting heavily forested areas have a particular difficulty in relying on the sun's rays to provide the warmth necessary to ensure the development of their eggs. Little direct heat will penetrate under a dense forest canopy, and so Schneider's dwarf caiman (*Paleosuchus trigonatus*) has evolved an unusual means of overcoming this problem, by laying its eggs in a nest at the base of a termite mound. The location of the nest relative to the mound is generally critical to the successful hatching of the eggs. Should it be located too close to the termites, then the temperature will be excessively high, while, obviously, if the eggs are located some distance away, then it will be too low.

It is now clear, however, that the female caiman will use the termites' nest simply as a source of auxiliary heat if she has nested in the vicinity previously. She may return to the site and simply add further material to her old nest. Even if the termite colony has died out in the interim, this arrangement should ensure that the eggs hatch successfully, because the old nest provides additional insulation, increasing the temperature in the layers above, where the eggs have been laid. As the embryos develop, so their metabolic heat is trapped within the nest, and growth of vegetation on the mound during the incubation period ensures that the interior remains suitably warm.

THE BREEDING PERIOD

As a nesting stimulus, ambient temperature appears especially important for crocodilians inhabiting sub-tropical areas. The rise in temperature during the spring is significant in this regard for the American alligator. A similar response can be seen in those populations of the Nile crocodile outside the tropics. Another factor of importance is rainfall, and the onset of the wet season stimulates reproductive behaviour.

Those Nile crocodiles at the southern end of their range nest only from the end of September through until the middle of December. Here, the climate does not permit successful breeding at any other time, except through the summer. Further north, however, within the tropics, where there is little variation in temperature, two distinct breeding periods are noted, which appear to be more related to rainfall. Nesting takes place between August and September, and December and January.

While the American alligator has a relatively short and well-defined breeding period, other species may nest over a much longer period. Indeed, Indo-Pacific crocodiles often lay for up to six months of the year. Each female only lays once, however, and this is the usual pattern for all crocodilians, except the mugger (*Crocodylus palustris*). Studies at the Madras Crocodile Bank in India have confirmed that as many as eight out of ten breeding females there will nest twice during the year. It may be that local environmental factors, such as a constant supply of food, have led to this phenomenon.

It is not unusual for a female to prepare trial nesting sites, and such is the case in the mugger and the gharial (*Gavialis gangeticus*), which both dig nests. In all cases, a site is generally chosen which will not be flooded, as this is likely to prove fatal for developing embryos. Gharials lay their eggs at least 3–5 m (10–16 ft) from the water's edge.

Even species which build nest mounds, thus raising the eggs further from the water level, choose a site where flooding is unlikely to occur. They may return to the area used in the previous year, but often prepare a new nest, slightly away from the original site. This is invariably a laborious task, which will take several days, and possibly up to a month, depending on the female's commitment.

Easy access to the chosen nesting site is important and, while Nile crocodiles may follow the trails of hippopotamuses from the water, American alligators will prepare a route, biting and scrabbling away the vegetation. A clear area, measuring perhaps 3×2.5 m (10×8 ft), provides the basis for the nest. In the centre of this area, vegetation is piled up, augmented with twigs, leaves and other debris, carried by the female in her mouth.

Nest-building takes place at night, with the mound being compressed by the weight of the female. The base can extend to about 2 m (6 ft), and is about 70 cm (28 in) high. Then the female may pause to excavate a hollow in the top of the mound, using her hind feet. This in turn may be filled with aquatic vegetation and mud gathered from the shallows.

Subsequently, another hole is excavated in amongst this debris, and it will be here that the female actually lays her eggs. This again takes

Plate 48   A major predator of crocodile eggs in Australia, the goanna digs up the nests, often distracting guarding females by operating in pairs. One lizard draws off the mother, while the other obtains the eggs.

place at night and, remarkably, once the process has started, she then appears to be unaware of other events in her immediate vicinity. At this stage, it is even possible to approach a female crocodilian and collect the eggs as they are laid, with virtually no risk of being attacked.

Female turtles will also tolerate a very close approach during the actual egg-laying period, after they have hauled themselves out of the water and excavated a nest. The reasons for this behaviour are unclear – it may simply be the most expedient means of completing the process, at a time when the reptiles are clearly vulnerable.

Most crocodilians lay their full clutch of eggs within 30 minutes, and then carefully cover the nest site, sometimes collecting a little more material for this purpose. The female is then likely to remain in the vicinity, watching over the nest. Some species prove more belligerent than others in this respect. The Indo-Pacific crocodile is particularly aggressive in defence of its nest and usually attacks any perceived intruder without hesitation. Others may give a warning, by hissing and lunging with an open mouth initially, and then attacking if this does not prove a satisfactory deterrent.

In the case of Johnston's crocodile, although the female may be nearby, she will make little effort to protect her nest. This behaviour varies according to the population. Generally, in areas where crocodilians have been extensively hunted, they tend to be less defensive at their nest sites, preferring instead to remain inconspicuous and avoid human contact.

Mugger crocodiles have a special burrow which they excavate near

Plate 49   The maribou stork (*Leptoptilos crumeniferus*) will readily feast on crocodile eggs and hatchlings in Africa, often probing through a nest site in order to locate them.

their nest, whereas other species dig a wallow, which is a muddy area close by, that fills with water. Female Nile crocodiles, in contrast, spend much of their time out of the water, lying close to their nest.

A number of potential predators will raid the nests of crocodilians. Large lizards, such as the Nile monitor (*Varanus niloticus*) and the goannas of Australia, represent a particular threat. Their powerful claws enable them to excavate a nest without difficulty. Crocodile eggs are also taken by mammals, including hyenas, mongooses and peccaries,

87

and even passing birds such as the maribou stork (*Leptoptilos crumeniferus*) will join in at an opened nest site if the opportunity presents itself.

While the physical presence of crocodiles will deter most predators from attacking the nests, the smaller caimans may find themselves under greater threat, because they are vulnerable to predators such as jaguars. But caiman nests generally do not suffer from flooding as often as those of larger species. This is a major cause of breeding failure, although American alligator eggs can be submerged for up to 12 hours before their hatchability is seriously compromised.

THE DEVELOPMENT OF THE EGG

Soon after mating has taken place, the ova, which are full of yolk, leave the female crocodilian's ovary. Fertilization occurs in the oviducts and, subsequently, the albumen fraction of the egg is added, followed by the leathery shell membrane, with the hard calcerous shell finally being deposited on top.

For the eggs in turn to hatch successfully, they must start by having all the necessary ingredients to sustain early embryonic development through to hatching. In the wild, crocodilians tend to feed on whole animals, including bones, and so are unlikely to suffer from nutritional imbalances which may arise in captive stock.

A diet of red meat, for example, with its low calcium : phosphorus ratio, of the order 1 : 44, means that laying females are liable to suffer from a calcium imbalance, which will probably manifest itself in soft-shelled eggs. In order to lay a clutch of up to 50 eggs or so, a female crocodilian will need to expend a considerable amount of her calcium reserves. Some of this may be drawn from the osteoderms, which can function as a labile store of calcium.

It is also clear from studies with captive crocodilians that Vitamin E is vital for good hatchability. Deficiencies typically result from a diet of large amounts of marine fish, whose oils contain damaging lipid per-oxides. While females may show no trace of a deficiency, a lower than normal level of Vitamin E in the egg will almost certainly result in the death of the embryo, since embryos are more sensitive than adults to this deficiency.

When they are laid, the eggs of crocodilians already contain relatively advanced embryos, which will have reached the 20-somite stage. But, unlike the situation in higher vertebrates, and some reptiles, the sex of the offspring is not already determined at this stage by genetic influences. Instead, this relies upon temperature-dependent sex determination, often known under its acronym of TSD.

The first evidence of this phenomenon in crocodilians was discovered in 1982 and was based on the results obtained from experiments with American alligators. In these experiments, the sex ratios of hatchlings from eggs which were incubated at a constant temperature in a laboratory were compared with those hatched from eggs from the field. It became apparent that many more males were being produced in the wild, compared with the situation in artificially incubated eggs. Further study then revealed that incubating the eggs at temperatures below 32°C (90°F) yielded a higher proportion of female offspring, whereas above this figure, males would be produced. The temperature band where both males and females were produced in equal proportions was just 1°C (2°F).

It seems clear that this pattern also applies to the Chinese alligator, as well as caimans. From investigations carried out to date, however, the situation is quite different in crocodilians. Temperatures below 31°C (88°F) and from 33–44°C (91–111°F) will yield female hatchlings, whereas males are produced if the eggs are incubated between these temperatures.

Since the temperature throughout a nest can vary by a relatively small amount, it is quite possible for eggs laid by a female crocodilian to produce offspring of different sexes, especially as they are not all buried at the same depth. Nevertheless, the site chosen by the female will probably have a significant bearing on the outcome. It may be that the trial nesting sites, often constructed before egg-laying takes place, may reflect an attempt by the female to choose the most advantageous site for the hatching of offspring of a predetermined sex. At the present stage, however, this area of crocodilian behaviour remains a mystery.

External factors also play a part, because, in spite of the attempts of the female crocodile to provide extra warmth for her eggs by burying them in a mound, the ambient temperature outside will determine ultimately whether or not they hatch. As might be expected, it seems that, generally, incubation conditions favour the production of female offspring. This is of survival significance for the species, since the more eggs which are laid, the greater the likelihood of adequate recruitment to the population to ensure its continuance. A single male crocodilian will mate with numerous females, so for reproductive purposes, there is no benefit in having a near equal sex ratio in the population.

Shifts in climatic patterns could potentially affect crocodilian populations, especially those outside the tropics, over a period of time. The obvious risk with TSD is that a fall or rise in temperature will result in offspring of a single sex being hatched from all nests. Over the course of perhaps a century, this could spell disaster for the species. It may explain past extinctions, and has been advanced as a reason for the disappearance of the dinosaurs. Clearly, however, if this is correct, crocodilians proved more adaptable in their breeding habits.

Spreading the nesting period over a longer season can help to eliminate minor climatic fluctuations, as seen by the case of the mugger today. Those which nest early in the year lay eggs which give rise mainly to female offspring, because the surroundings are then relatively cool. In contrast, females laying later produce nests with more male offspring, simply because the sun's rays have warmed the soil by this stage.

Research into TSD is continuing, but already it is clear that conservationists now have a highly significant tool for the purposes of a captive breeding programme. Working with only a few eggs, it is possible to maximize the production of female offspring simply by adjusting the incubation temperature. For many of the endangered species, this offers great hope for their survival.

HATCHING

There is no fixed incubation period for the eggs of crocodilians, although the majority will hatch between two and three months of

Plate 50   This tiny Nile crocodile (*Crocodylus niloticus*) hatchling is barely 25 cm (10 in) long, but could prove to be a man-eater when it grows up.

Plate 51   At this stage, hatchling crocodiles face a whole range of predators, and few will survive the crucial early years of life.

Plate 52   Young crocodilians often follow a different diet to adults, so avoiding direct competition for food. This caiman is feeding on fish.

being laid. The critical period for sex determination is early during the incubation process, extending from the seventh to the twenty-first day. Failure to hatch can be caused by flooding of the nest, or exposure of the eggs to adverse temperatures, typically below 27°C (81°F) or about 34°C (93°F). Alternatively, they may simply not have been fertilized.

The instincts of the female to guard the nest may lessen during the incubation period, possibly because the site itself becomes less conspicuous to predators. But in the majority of cases, she will be in close proximity when the eggs are ready to hatch. The acute hearing of crocodilians ensures that the cries of the youngsters will be audible to the listening female just before they start to break out of their eggs.

In some cases, her presence can be absolutely critical to their survival. The eggs of Schneider's dwarf caiman, laid in close proximity to a termite mound, may actually be incorporated into the structure of the nest during the incubation period. Trapped in the interior, the hatchlings would be unable to escape into the outside world unless their mother was nearby to break open the hard walls of the termite chamber.

Young crocodilians are at risk from many predators, and the journey from the nest site to the water is potentially extremely perilous. Again, this threat is minimized by the presence of their mother. Once one or two youngsters have started their high-pitched barking from within the nest, others follow, and the resulting noise may be audible from 15 m (16 yd) away. This will stimulate her to open the nest.

The hatchlings are tightly curled within the shell by this stage, with their heads and tails twisted around their bellies. On the tip of the snout, there is an egg-tooth or caruncle. This is not a tooth in the real sense, but a sharp projection of skin which enables the young crocodilian to slice into the leathery shell membrane and break through the egg shell. By this stage, the shell itself is somewhat thinner than at the time of laying, because calcium and other minerals have been absorbed into the hatchling's body during its development. In addition, bacteria in the soil will weaken the shell structure, facilitating the break-out of the hatchlings.

The length of the young crocodilian is considerably greater than that of the egg by this stage. In the case of the American alligator, for example, the average length of the egg is about 6 cm ($2\frac{1}{2}$ in), whereas the hatchling will be approximately 21.5 cm ($8\frac{1}{2}$ in) from the tip of its snout to its tail. On emerging from the egg, the young crocodilian's belly will be considerably distended by the remains of the yolk sac, which nourished it through the incubation period.

The absorption of this yolk continues during the early part of the young crocodilian's life, so that it can adjust to its new environment without needing to obtain food at this critical stage. The slight scar left at the site of the yolk sac attachment will last much longer, however, and will be visible for some months. The 'egg-tooth' itself is reabsorbed into the body within about a week, having served its purpose.

Some females actively assist the hatching process, by carefully crushing the eggs in their mouths, and freeing the young crocodilians from the shells. But even in the absence of their mother, hatchlings can break out of the nest themselves. This has been noted in parts of the alligator's range in the USA, where adult females have been shot at their nesting sites, and yet their young emerge later, and head straight for water.

Experiments have shown that, in the first instance, recently hatched alligators have a strong tendency to move from a dark area to a brighter locality. This obviously encourages them to leave the nest. They also show a strong affinity for conditions of high humidity, which may enable them to locate water without difficulty.

If the female is in the vicinity, she will often carry her offspring carefully to the water, in her mouth. In the case of the mugger, the male has also been known to act in this way, even to the extent of assisting hatchlings from their eggs.

THE GROWTH OF HATCHLINGS

Adults helping youngsters through these early stages of life are usually very aggressive towards any potential intruders. The hatchlings them-selves are also equipped with sharp teeth in their jaws, and will not hesitate to bite if threatened in any way. They often stay together in groups, called pods, during these early days, and continue to be quite vocal. This alerts other crocodilians to their presence and any per-ceived danger. A female will usually respond in defence of her off-spring, even once they are in water. They may also be seen staying close to her, resting on her back for periods of the day.

Members of a pod remain in the same locality for as long as two years, although by this stage, in spite of their mother's endeavours, their numbers will have been considerably reduced by predation. Large wading birds, including various herons, will seek them out in the shallows, while on land, ground hornbills, wild cats and mountain lizards prey on them. In deeper water, catfish, otters and turtles are just some of the potential dangers which young crocodilians face. They may also be consumed by other, older, crocodilians.

During their first winter, American alligators often seek safe retreats, such as an existing den, rather than risk being frozen in an open area of water. Assuming they can find adequate food and escape predators,

Plate 53   Reared in artificial surroundings, the growth rate of young crocodilians is invariably better than that of wild stock. Ultimately, males will continue to grow at a faster rate than females and will be correspondingly larger.

Plate 54   Studies on the rearing of crocodilians have revealed that keeping them in warm surroundings, with a regular supply of food, will dramatically enhance their growth rates, with no apparent adverse effects. Much of this research has resulted from international interest in crocodilian farming and ranching techniques.

young crocodilians will grow surprisingly rapidly. By 1 year old, they will have nearly tripled in size, to approximately 61 cm (24 in) in the case of alligator hatchlings. They should grow another 30 cm (12 in) over the course of the next 12 months, reaching about 111 cm (44 in) during their third year. At 4 years old, their juvenile phase is past. They now cease to call like juveniles and start to bellow instead, having lived through the most dangerous part of their lives.

Their growth rate will slow down noticeably by the time they are about 8 years old and approaching 2.4 m (8 ft) in length. From this stage onwards, American alligators will continue growing, but less evidently, until they are at least 25 years old. Often, after this stage, their growth is imperceptible. Females, as has been mentioned previously, have a slower growth rate than males once the initial juvenile surge has passed, and remain smaller throughout their lives.

Chapter 5

The Evolution and Distribution of Crocodilians

Crocodilians are the sole survivors from the ruling age of reptiles, whose ancestry dates back to the Mesozoic era, about 265 million years ago. They belong to the Archosauria group, which includes both the dinosaurs and pterosaurs. Although these life forms vanished around the end of the Cretaceous period, some 66 million years ago, the lineage of crocodilians retaining the characteristic features of the group has continued through to the present day.

The most conspicuous of these is the imbalance in length between the fore and hind limbs, with the latter being notably longer. But, internally, there is also an additional opening, called the antorbital fenestra, located in front of the eye sockets on each side of the skull.

The reason for this feature is unclear, but it is generally assumed to be linked with the musculature responsible for closing the relatively long jaws. It has now essentially vanished in contemporary crocodilians, but can be traced through the early lineage of these reptiles, confirming their relationship with other archosaurs.

Fig. 2   An evolutionary pathway, based on that devised by Wilfred T. Neill.

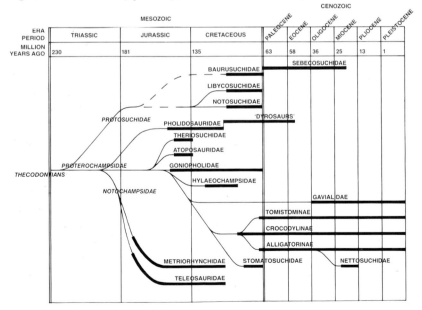

THE EVOLUTION OF CROCODILIANS

THE ORIGINS OF CROCODILIANS

In the early part of the Mesozoic era, there was a primitive group of reptiles called thecodontians. Their name originates from their dentition, in which the teeth were set in sockets rather than being attached simply to the jaw bones. The teeth themselves were hollow, with replacements developing beneath, in the individual sockets.

The thecodontians first appeared during the Permian period, at the start of the Mesozoic era, and rapidly diversified during the subsequent Triassic period. They were generally quite small creatures, able to live in water as well as on land, and often had a protective body covering in the form of bony plates. Indeed, it appears that the earliest ancestors of contemporary crocodilians were terrestrial rather than aquatic by nature.

Their earliest known relatives are described collectively as sphenosuchians and the oldest form, called *Gracilisuchus*, was discovered in Argentina. Growing to about 30 cm (12 in) in length, this creature would, at first sight, have shown little obvious similarity to today's crocodilians.

Indeed, until the start of the 1980s, it was grouped as a member of the ornithosuchian dinosaurs. It probably had a bipedal gait, with a long tail and slender hind limbs, and could, presumably, run quite effectively. But *Gracilisuchus* also had large, powerful jaws and studies of the anatomy of its head and neck confirm its relationship with crocodilians.

In addition, its ankle joints had an unusual structure still apparent in present-day crocodilians. This probably means that it also could move in two ways on land. When covering relatively large distances, *Gracilisuchus* would walk rather like a mammal, with a relatively long stride length. This would enable it to move at speed. Yet, apparently, *Gracilisuchus* could also walk with its underparts close to the ground and its legs slung out rather at right angles to its body. This may suggest that *Gracilisuchus* was not entirely bipedal, but could alternate its gait according to circumstances.

Crocodilians today retain a dual mode of quadruped locomotion, which is achieved by a similar structure in their ankle joints. Under normal circumstances, in other reptiles, the ankle joint itself is located in a straight line between the proximal (upper) and distal (lower) bones. In crocodilians, however, the joint is positioned between the two proximal bones, which alternate with different parts of the limb.

The tibia (shin bone) and fibula (brooch bone) of the leg are linked with the astragalus (ankle bone), while the calcaneum (heel bone)

97

actually forms part of the foot. It articulates with the astragalus via a hollow socket, into which a protrusion of the astragalus fits. This in turn provides the necessary support when the crocodile moves its legs outwards and proceeds to walk in a more upright fashion.

Gracilisuchus itself was protected from predators by a double row of bony plates. These ran along its back, down the tail. This sphenosuchian is thought to have hunted small lizards, which is grabbed in its powerful jaws, lined with backward-pointing teeth, which would have made a formidable weapon.

A slimmer, more streamlined version of *Gracilisuchus* was *Terrestrisuchus*, which evolved later, towards the end of the Triassic period, about 210 million years ago. Although measuring 50 cm (20 in) in total length, its tail was twice the combined length of its head and body. The limbs of *Terrestrisuchus* were also longer than those of *Gracilisuchus* and terminated in short claws.

It appears to have been a quadruped, but may also have run on two feet as well, catching both lizards and insects in its elongated jaws, which bear more than a passing resemblance to those of crocodiles. The remains of *Terrestrisuchus* have been unearthed in Wales, and it is assumed to have ranged over much of present-day Europe. The sphenosuchians are generally accepted as being the closest direct relatives of today's crocodiles.

But contemporaneously with *Terrestrisuchus*, there was a group of aquatic carnivores which, by the close of the Triassic period, had evolved an appearance very similar to that of crocodilians. Known as phytosaurs, these were also of thecodontian stock, and were widely distributed throughout the rivers of both North America and Europe. They grew up to 5 m (16 ft) in length, and fed on fish, and probably other smaller reptiles as well.

One of the best-known phytosaurs is *Rutioden*, which had a long narrow snout filled with teeth, and was probably not unlike the gharial of today. It measured 3 m (10 ft) in length. But the characteristic feature which sets phytosaurs apart from crocodilians is the positioning of their nostrils. These were located, not at the end of the snout, but close to the eye sockets, while, internally, phytosaurs also lacked a secondary palate.

It appears that this particular evolutionary line was lost at the end of the Triassic period, with the phytosaurs themselves being a clear example of parallel evolution. They developed to fill the same evolutionary niche as that occupied by crocodilians today, although they played no part in the development of this group.

Another late Triassic reptile with an appearance not dissimilar to that of a crocodile was *Desmatosuchus*, which is known to have occurred in the southern part of the USA. It grew to 5 m (16 ft) in length, and had a heavily armoured body, which included spines measuring up to 45 cm (18 in) long, projecting horizontally backwards from its shoulders.

These aetosaurs had the type of ankle joint associated with crocodilians today. Yet it is clear from a study of its dentition that *Desmatosuchus* was a herbivore and, again, this particular group died out at the end of the Triassic period.

There were other crocodile-like reptiles also living on the land at this stage. They included the various rauisuchians, which could grow up to 6 m (20 ft) in length. A typical example of the group was *Ticinosuchus*, known to have occurred in Europe. It reached a size of about 3 m (10 ft) and, in this case, the hind legs were positioned beneath the body, rather than protruding sideways as in older thecodontians.

Rauisuchians appear to have reached their greatest diversity in South America. They were quadrupeds, with an ankle structure similar to that associated with present-day crocodilians. Their bodies were protected by interlocking plates which ran down their backs, while their jaws contained a fearsome array of sharp teeth, capable of ripping their prey apart.

Interestingly, one of the earliest thecodontian groups, whose ancestry dates back to the preceding Permian period, included both aquatic and terrestrial members. These proterosuchians included *Chasmatosaurus*, whose remains have been unearthed in both southern Africa and China. Reaching about 2 m ($6\frac{1}{2}$ ft) in length, *Chasmatosaurus* is believed to have lived predominantly in rivers, preying on fish.

The tip of its upper jaw curved down sharply over its lower jaw, with pointed, backward-curved teeth filling the mouth. These extended on to the palate in this case. Resembling a cross between a lizard and crocodile in appearance, *Chasmatosaurus* was also able to walk on land. Its legs were positioned at right angles to its body, with five toes on each foot.

Other predatory proterosuchians could be found on land. These included *Erythrosuchus*, which has also been discovered in southern Africa. Growing to about 4.5 m (15 ft) in total length, its head alone was nearly 1 m ($3\frac{1}{2}$ ft) long, confirming its predatory status, as its jaws were filled with numerous sharp teeth. It had a more upright gait than *Chasmatosaurus*.

The relationship of the proterosuchians to other thecodontians is unclear. It may be that they were the original ancestral form. Certainly when they became extinct at the close of the Triassic period, the proterosuchians had achieved a worldwide distribution, but it was to be the sphenosuchian lineage which continued through to the subsequent

Jurassic period, and ultimately yielded the forms which gave rise to today's crocodilians.

CONTINUING EVOLUTION

Members of the suborder Protosuchia still lived on land, like their sphenosuchian ancestors, and had long legs. Significant modifications of their skull structure are apparent, however, and begin to resemble those of true crocodilians. *Protosuchus* clearly spent most, if not all, of its time on land, as its remains have been found in North America in the company of terrestrial dinosaurs.

In this case, the jaw structure shows signs of modification, becoming significantly wider at the back of the skull. This would have enabled *Protosuchus* to have both a wide gape and powerful muscles responsible for closing the jaws. As with today's crocodilians, prominent canine teeth in the lower jaw were effectively concealed by corresponding notches in the upper jaw, and *Protosuchus* would have been a formidable predator.

It is generally thought that at least some protosuchians showed early signs of the development of a secondary palate. This is a critical feature of today's crocodilians and enables them to open their mouths under water while continuing to breathe through their nostrils.

But, in the protosuchians, the secondary palate was certainly not ossified. Instead, it was probably formed by the backward growth of the maxillae and palatines, completed by a fleshy cartilaginous membrane.

The descendants of the protosuchians, which emerged quite early during the Jurassic period, also show this vital adaptation to obtaining prey in water. These were the mesosuchians, a large group divided into 16 families, which are thought to have comprised over 70 genera.

Many still lived on land, such as the sebecids, a fearsome group of predators present in South American as recently as 65 million years ago. These reptiles nevertheless had a recognizable crocodilian appearance, and their scientific name was derived from Sebek, the crocodile god of ancient Egypt. It seems likely that they could have been the dominant predators in South America at this stage, before the arrival of carnivorous mammals on what was then an island continent.

MARINE CROCODILIANS (THALATTOSUCHIANS)

Of the various mesosuchian families, it appears that just four were predominantly aquatic in their habits. Members of the Teleosauridae evolved in rather a similar way to the gharial, with long, narrow snouts.

They lived in the oceans, feeding on fish and invertebrates such as squid.

One of the best-known examples of this family is *Teleosaurus*, which grew to about 3 m (10 ft) in length. Its body was very streamlined, and its short front legs were almost certainly held against the sides of the body as it swam.

Teleosaurus moved through the water by powerful movements of its tail, rather like a present-day lizard. Nevertheless, these early crocodilians still ventured on to land to lay their eggs, probably frequenting the small islands which formed much of the area of Europe at the time.

Some crocodilians were to become even better adapted to a marine existence as the Jurassic period continued. They included members of the Metriorhynchidae family. These achieved a wide distribution throughout the world's oceans, and their remains have been discovered in localities as far apart as Europe and Chile. As the family evolved during the later part of the Jurassic period, the protective body armour, seen in *Teleosaurus*, was sacrificed for increased mobility in the sea.

One of the earlier examples was *Metriorhynchus*, which grew to about 3 m (10 ft) in length. The limbs in this case altered significantly in appearance, becoming converted into paddles. The rear flippers were narrow and longer, suggesting that they may have had a locomotive role.

In addition, the rear of the vertebral column gave rise to an effective tail fin, which was vertical rather than horizontal in shape. The caudal vertebrae themselves curved sharply downwards for this purpose, and these crocodilians swam mainly by means of lateral tail movements.

Although clearly at home in the oceans, the metriorhynchids would undoubtedly have encountered considerable difficulty in moving on land. It is tempting to suggest that, like certain sea snakes today, they may have become ovoviviparous.

Alternatively, they would have had to haul themselves up on to beaches to lay their eggs, like marine turtles. It is possible that their hind limbs could have been used to excavate a nest for this purpose, but at present, their reproductive habits remain a mystery. What is known, however, is that, in the case of the contemporary ichthyosaurs, which adopted a similar marine lifestyle, reproduction was achieved by ovoviviparous means, and this remains the most likely possibility for metriorhynchids as well.

Even more specialized forms, such as *Geosaurus*, were to evolve towards the end of the Jurassic period. The remains of this marine crocodile have been found in both Europe and South America.

The deviation of the vertebral column into the lower portion of the

Plate 55   Crocodilians that are highly aquatic have a very streamlined shape, like their ancestors.

tail fin was far more pronounced in this instance. Neural spines, directed cranially towards the head, provided greater support for the fin, which was also larger than that of *Metriorhynchus*. This presumably meant that *Geosaurus* could swim more effectively, and was probably a more efficient predator.

The specialized lifestyle of these marine crocodiles, which are sometimes described collectively as thalattosuchians, probably contributed to their extinction early during the subsequent Cretaceous period, about 145 million years ago. At this time the shallow seas which had covered most of Europe began to dry up and the holostean fish, on which the thalattosuchians preyed, also fell in numbers, while today's teleost fish became more numerous.

Fossilized remains have provided tantilizing insights into the lifestyles of these marine crocodilians. A huge fish, called *Leedsichthys*, which could grow to nearly 6 m (20 ft) long, was apparently a favoured prey of *Metriorhynchus*. Clearly, thalattosuchians hunted creatures much larger than themselves.

Recent discoveries in deposits of Oxford clay in England have confirmed that *Metriorhynchus* was also something of an opportunist predator. Its stomach contents have been found to include the remains of cephalopods and possibly the bones of a pterosaur, which may well have been caught as it skimmed over the surface of the sea in search of fish.

THE EVOLUTIONARY IMPORTANCE OF SMALL MESOSUCHIANS

Some mesosuchians represented neither the terrestrial lifestyle exemplified by the later sebecosuchians, nor the totally aquatic existence of the thalattosuchians. One of the best-known members of this group is *Bernissartia*, a small species whose remains have been discovered in

Plate 56   It is still possible to detect similarities between contemporary crocodilians and the early mesosuchians that were their direct ancestors.

Europe. It grew to just 1 m ($3\frac{1}{4}$ ft) in length, and frequented the huge but shallow Wealden Lake, which extended from the south-east of England as far as Belgium, about 130 million years ago.

Bernissartia was well protected by its body armour and was a relatively advanced mesosuchian. The area of bone behind the eye socket had sunk below the surface of the skull, a feature associated with crocodilians today.

The teeth in the front of its mouth were relatively narrow and sharp, and may have been used for grabbing fish and other prey. Those further back in the jaws have a flatter, broader appearance, which may have enabled these crocodilians to feed on shellfish, or possibly carrion obtained on land.

Even smaller crocodilians, little bigger than many contemporary lizards, are known from the late Jurassic and early Cretaceous periods. The atoposaurids had short snouts, and appear to have been predominantly terrestrial in their habits. They were agile, with relatively long legs and large eyes.

The largest known atoposaurid is *Alligatorium*, which grew to just 40 cm (16 in) long. Like other members of the family, its remains have been found mainly in Europe. It appears that the Atoposauridae were not represented on the southern land mass, although the family did extend to both North America and Asia.

One of the most significant atoposaurid finds was made at Swanage, in Dorset, England. *Theriosuchus* may have marked an evolutionary stage onwards towards the eusuchians, or modern crocodiles. It reflects the beginning of the involvement of the pterygoids in the formation of a secondary palate.

In addition, its vertebrae show signs of transformation from the amphicoelous type associated with early crocodilians to the procoelous form characteristic of modern eusuchians. Procoelous vertebrae, based on a ball and socket design, permit greater flexibility of movement, compared with the more rigid structure of an amphicoelous vertebrae. Later examples of *Theriosuchus*, from the early Cretaceous period, show entirely procoelous vertebrae.

GONIOPHOLIDS AND THEIR RELATIVES

While atoposaurid crocodiles are assumed to have played a significant part in the continuing development of the crocodilian line, there are those who believe that another group, known as the goniopholids, is significant in this respect.

Members of the family Goniopholididae were much larger in size than the atoposaurids, and possessed a relatively broad and elongated snout. They were probably rather similar in appearance to contemporary crocodilians, although again, they lacked a proper secondary palate. These mesosuchians were well protected both dorsally, by interconnecting scutes, and ventrally, by a protective shield.

Goniopholids were essentially found on the northern Laurasian land mass. Their range extended as far east as Thailand, at the end of the Jurassic period, and the family was also represented across western Europe and North America.

Goniopholis crassidens was a typical example, with a skull about 60 cm (24 in) long, housing about 23 pairs of teeth in its jaws. Others, such as *Goniopholis simus*, were smaller, with this particular species not exceeding 2.1 m (7 ft) in overall length. These crocodilians lived in marshy or relatively shallow areas of water and took a variety of prey.

The pholidosaurids were similar to the goniopholids, but had narrower snouts. Their distribution was also more widespread, with the giant form *Sarcosuchus* being found in both South America and Africa. In this species, the skull alone measured over 2 m (6 ft), and the total body length was probably about 11 m (36 ft). These appear to have been freshwater crocodilians, although *Teleorhinus* frequented the shallow seas which covered much of present-day North America towards the end of the Cretaceous period.

At this stage, another group of long-snouted crocodilians, known as the dyrosaurs had begun to appear, and spread predominantly through the Southern Hemisphere. These appear to have been a fish-eating species, like *Dyrosaurus* itself, and they were particularly common in North Africa.

Phosphatosaurus was one of the largest members of this family, reaching a length of approximately 9 m (30 ft). The teeth in the rear of its jaws were flattened, and it is possible that it preyed to some extent on marine turtles, crushing their shells with these powerful teeth.

The dyrosaurids were found in the Tethys Sea, which covered a wide area, separating the northern and southern continents. These particular crocodilians also crossed the Atlantic Ocean to the eastern coast of North America, although this was then a much shorter distance than it is today. Their remains have also been found in South America, close to the shores of Lake Titicaca in Bolivia.

THE EUSUCHIANS

Although their precise ancestry is still unclear, the origins of present-day crocodilians date back to the end of the Jurassic period. They developed from mesosuchians, which themselves also survived into the subsequent Cretaceous period, after the extinction of the dinosaurs.

105

Plate 57   The lifestyle of crocodilians as a group may not have changed significantly in some respects for millions of years.

It is likely that the original eusuchians were partly aquatic, lurking in relatively shallow areas of water, such as rivers and swamps. Their large heads and powerful jaws made them a match for much larger prey, which could be dragged under water and drowned, before being consumed.

Unfortunately, the fossil history of crocodilians still contains notable gaps, especially in the mid-Cretaceous period. But it is clear that the direct forerunners of today's crocodilians had clearly evolved during the late Cretaceous period about 80 million years ago.

Included amongst their number was *Deinosuchus*, whose name translates as 'terrible crocodile'. It is sometimes also known as *Phobosuchus* or 'horror crocodile', which is another reference to its vast size. At the present time, only a virtually complete skull of *Deinosuchus* has been found, so it is impossible to be certain of its overall length. But, working on an equivalent ratio with other crocodilians, and bearing in mind that its skull alone measured over 2 m ($6\frac{1}{2}$ ft), it is probable that *Deinosuchus* exceeded 15.2 m (50 ft) from snout to tail. This huge size probably enabled *Deinosuchus* to prey on quite large dinosaurs, which it grabbed as they passed near its hidden lair.

However, a contrasting school of thought sees these crocodilians as having had a significantly large head relative to their body length, and suggests they were primarily terrestrial rather than semi-aquatic, but this view is not widely accepted.

106

Deinosuchus was almost certainly quite widespread over much of the present-day USA. Each of its vertebrae alone are believed to have measured up to 30 cm (12 in) long, and its body weight would have exceeded 6 tonnes. *Deinosuchus* may have preyed mainly on the various duck-billed dinosaurs, characterized by strange head embellishments, which are known as hadrosaurs. The fossils of both tend to be found in the company of each other.

Certainly later eusuchian crocodilians did not lose their affinity for land. Some even remained predominantly, if not totally, terrestrial in their habits. They included *Pristichampus*, which grew to about 3 m (10 ft) in length. Its legs were adapted for running, and it had hooves rather than claws on its feet.

Pristichampus also had sharp teeth, very similar in structure to those of the great predatory dinosaurs, such as *Tyrannosaurus*. Indeed, palaeontologists confused their origins at first, and this led to suggestions that these dinosaurs had survived the mass Cretaceous extinctions, and lived until comparatively recently. In fact, *Pristichampus* evolved during the Eocene epoch, around 50 million years ago, and preyed on the mammals which had become the dominant life form at this stage.

This group of crocodilians appears to have died out in the Northern Hemisphere towards the close of the Eocene epoch. But they certainly survived much longer in the Southern Hemisphere and, in Australia, remains of such crocodilians are as recent as the Pleistocene epoch, barely two million years ago.

The eusuchians have actually declined in numbers since their evolution, mainly for climatic reasons. While the basic division seen today, separating crocodiles from alligators, took place by 80 million years ago, the immediate ancestors of these eusuchians are unclear. Nevertheless, a clue to their common ancestral stock may be provided by the New Caledonian crocodile (*Mekosuchus inexpectatus*). It is the only known species in the family Mekosuchidae, discovered as recently as 1980. These particular crocodilians died out just 1700 years ago. They retained some clear characteristics associated with the mesosuchians, yet also had much in common with today's eusuchians.

The New Caledonian crocodile is thought to have evolved around the close of the Cretaceous period, some 65 million years ago. At this stage, New Caledonia was still joined to Australia. It is possible that the New Caledonian crocodile could have evolved here from pristichampine stock, and may have survived because of the absence of competing species.

The remains of *Quinkana fortirostrum* show this species to be the most recent of the pristichampine crocodilians yet unearthed on this continent. Almost certainly, it survived because of the isolation of Australia, where prey was abundant, but no specialist mammalian predators were established.

The pristichampines were crocodilians that had forsaken life in water, and become adapted to fill a specific ecological niche on land. When they finally died out, it was probably as a result of hunting by the earliest settlers, although a cooling climate may also have played a part.

Nearer the equator, the New Caledonian crocodile would have been less at risk from climatic variation. Like the Australian pristicham-pines, it was a terrestrial species, which grew to a maximum size of 2 m ($6\frac{1}{2}$ ft), with well-developed limb muscles, as revealed by the attach-ment sites on the bones. Its diet is thought to have been based on molluscs, and its rear teeth are rounded, presumably for crushing shells.

It appears that this crocodilian was exterminated by the hunting activities of the very earliest human invaders of New Caledonia. It vanished first from the nearby Isle of Pines, according to the limited information available, and then from New Caledonia itself, before the arrival of European explorers.

Various crocodilians, such as the Philippine, or Mindoro, crocodile (*Crocodylus mindorensis*) are confined to small island areas today, but the unique feature of the New Caledonian crocodile was its terrestrial life-style. It may be that other similar species, thought to be extinct, still wait to be discovered on neighbouring islands.

THE SURVIVAL OF CROCODILIANS
The close of the Cretaceous period saw dramatic changes in the life forms present on the earth. The dinosaurs and a host of other, smaller, creatures died out for reasons which are not fully understood. Yet two reptilian groups, the crocodilians and the turtles, survived this appar-ent ecological catastrophe without suffering a dramatic decline in their numbers.

It is possible that their food chains were less disrupted by the events of that time. A fall-off in the vegetative cover of the planet would have spelt disaster for the large herbivorous dinosaurs and, in turn, the species which preyed on them. In the world's oceans, a reduction in the fish population would have dramatically affected ichthyosaurs and similar creatures, causing their ultimate extinction. But crocodilians have tended to be rather opportunistic feeders, and hence would have been more adaptable.

Climatic changes may also have played a part in this mass extinc-tion, but both crocodilians and turtles could possibly have survived a fall in the mean annual temperature by hibernating, as the American alligator (*Alligator mississippiensis*) does today.

It has been suggested that any fall in temperature would have compromised the reproductive capabilities of crocodilians, especially as they undergo temperature-dependent sex determination during the incubation period (see page 88). They would be vulnerable as a consequence because their eggs would then yield hatchlings of only one sex, causing the ultimate demise of the species over a period of time.

But as is clear from studies of present-day crocodilians, they choose their nesting sites with care, and raise the temperature within the nest by adding decomposing vegetation. It can therefore be argued that the lifestyle of crocodilians would not necessarily have suffered unduly from a change in the environmental temperature, compared with the less adaptable dinosaurs.

DISTRIBUTION OF CROCODILIANS

When crocodilians started to evolve during the Triassic period, there was just a single massive continent, known as Pangaea. Subsequently, this divided into the northern continent of Laurasia and its southern counterpart, called Gondwanaland, in the Jurassic period. This gradual change saw the start of individual populations beginning to evolve on different lines, as they became isolated with the further break-up of the continental land masses.

Clear evidence of this phenomenon can be seen from a study of the evolution of the crocodilian populations of present-day African and South America during the Cretaceous period. At the outset, when these continents were closely linked via the bulge of Africa, similar species could be found on both land masses. The remains of members of the family Notosuchidae, a group of small crocodilians with short snouts, such as *Araipesuchus*, have been unearthed both in the north-west of Africa and in Brazil, on the opposite side of the Atlantic Ocean.

Later, while the land masses were separating, such movement of fauna could no longer take place without great difficulty, although it is clear that a few crocodilians, such as the dyrosaurids, were able to cross the developing Atlantic Ocean right up until the start of the Tertiary period, about 65 million years ago.

Once the clear division became apparent between the two continents, however, the individual crocodilian populations of Africa and South America began to diverge, around 100 million years ago. The descendants of *Araipesuchus* gave rise to the family Notosuchidae in South America. These crocodilians have noticeably larger eye sockets and a reduced number of teeth, compared with *Araipesuchus*. Another

109

member of the family, *Uruguaysuchus*, shows even clearer evidence of its reduced dentition, and is adapted for a terrestrial mode of life.

In Africa, however, the lineage from *Araipesuchus* led to the family Libycosuchidae, whose remains have been found in Egypt. At present, only one species, christened *Libycosuchus brevirostris*, has been identified. This was characterized by having massive jaw muscles, but was still relatively small in terms of its overall size. Unlike most crocodilians, its teeth were positioned very close together.

The effects of continental drift have even affected the distribution of today's crocodilians, as exemplified by the case of the gharial (*Gavialis gangeticus*). It is believed that the origins of this specialist fish-eating crocodilian can be traced back to the old southern continent of Gondwanaland.

When this vast land mass broke up, part of its drifted north, fusing with Asia and producing the Himalayan Mountains as a consequence. An ancestral form of the gharial moved north on this island, passing close to Africa. It is likely that the group may have radiated briefly on to this continent, although conditions here do not appear to have been favourable. Perhaps competition from the huge pholidosaurids, which were also long-snouted, meant that they were unable to establish themselves effectively. In due course, however, the land mass, now known as India, joined with Asia, having conveyed its cargo of southern crocodilians across the equator to their new home.

Support for the radiation of gavialine stock comes from the finding of a totally new genus of crocodilians with long snouts in the area of Egypt. Their fossilized remains, dating back as far as the Eocene epoch, about 57 million years ago, show some clear similarities with today's gharials.

But there are also certain differences, such as the reduced pattern of dentition, and, most significantly, the fact that the nasal bones extend to separate the maxillae and continue forward to the premaxillae. This particular anatomical feature is associated rather with the false gharial (*Tomistoma schlegelii*) rather than *Gavialis* itself.

The discovery of the remains of *Eogavialis* does not resolve the mystery, however, but could prove evidence of a diverging population, resulting from the passage of India northwards. Since the remains of fossil gavialines from South America are more primitive than those found further north, this is somewhat compelling evidence that the group originated in this latter locality.

Alternatively, it has now been suggested that gavialines may have originated in the vicinity of Egypt, tracking westwards across the continent and then finally reaching South America. Here their evolution effectively ceased, while, in an easterly direction, the population became more specialized. This explanation seems less than satisfactory but, as in all fields of palaeontology, the possibility remains that further discoveries have yet to be made, which may resolve the situation.

The majority of these early gavialines were denizens of shallow coastal waters, whereas the gharial today is a freshwater crocodilian. Climatic changes around five million years ago saw the shallow northern seas dry up, and so these particular crocodilians generally faded into the fossil record. Some adapted to a freshwater environment, however, with *Tomistoma* surviving in parts of Africa as well as Asia, where the false gharial (*Tomistoma schlegelii*) is still found today. The genus disappeared in Africa, however, about two million years ago, for reasons which are unclear.

PRESENT DISTRIBUTION PATTERNS

A reduction in the number of species of crocodilians has taken place since the beginning of the Oligocene epoch, about 38 million years ago. Declining temperatures in Europe led to their extinction here, and generally, their range is now concentrated in tropical and sub-tropical areas of the world.

No longer are there any surviving terrestrial species. These have succumbed in the face of mammalian competition, and this has also

Plate 58   The origins of the American alligator (*Alligator mississippiensis*) can be traced back at least 57 million years.

clearly had an effect on the overall distribution of the group. Yet, right up until the extinction of the New Caledonian crocodile, for probably 200 million years, there had been terrestrial, predominantly aquatic and semi-aquatic species, reflecting the ecological adaptability of these reptiles.

Their diversity has been further emphasized by their ability to colonize both fresh and salt water. The Indo-Pacific crocodile (*Crocodylus porosus*) in particular maintains this salt-water link through to the present day. But now, the interrelationship between crocodilians and people will have a greater impact on their immediate future than any other evolutionary pressure in the past.

THE ORIGINS OF PRESENT-DAY ALLIGATORS AND CAIMANS

Although there are still significant gaps in the fossil record leading to today's alligators, their development in America is relatively well documented. The earliest Tertiary remains from North America date back to the Palaeocene epoch, around 57 million years ago. Here, in North Dakota, a small alligatorine, with a short and rather pointed snout, has been unearthed. Known as *Wannaganosuchus*, it was evidently well protected by scutes. Another Palaeocene find is that of *Ceratosuchus*, from Colorado. This alligatorine had strange head armaments, in the form of triangular horns, which resulted from an enlargement of the squamosal bones located at the back of the skull, behind the eyes. The function of these horns is unclear. They varied in length between individuals of the same size, and so it is possible that males might have had larger horns than females, perhaps using them in combat.

During the succeeding Eocene epoch, there were at least four different genera of alligatorine present in North America. These include *Allognathosuchus*, a relatively small species, growing up to 3 m (9¾ ft) in length. Its remains have also been found in Europe, where alligators were quite widespread at this stage. The unusually flattened and large rear teeth of the alligatorine, coupled with its powerful jaws, suggests that it may have preyed on turtles or shellfish.

While *Allognathosuchus* appears to have played no part in the development of contemporary alligators, it is possible that its descendants gave rise to the South American genus *Eocaiman*. These alligatorines are assumed to have been part of the ancestral line leading to contemporary caimans.

The most likely Eocene genus involved in the subsequent evolution of the various North American forms of alligator is *Procaimanoidea*. Its remains have been unearthed in Wyoming and in Utah. Again, its

112

dentition suggests that it fed on food which had to be crushed before swallowing. The head also was enlarged.

The fourth alligatorine genus known from the Eocene epoch in North America was *Diplocynodon*, but it seems to have a rather brief history, occurring here about 47 million years ago. In contrast, across the Atlantic in Europe, it survived until as recently as $3\frac{1}{2}$ million years ago, and its remains have been found over a wide area, from Spain to Bulgaria. This alligatorine is characterized by the presence of a double pair of caniniform teeth in its upper jaw.

Following the close of the Eocene epoch, the first member of the contemporary genus *Alligator* appeared during the succeeding Oligocene epoch, which lasted for 14 million years. Christened *Alligator prenasalis*, it lived in the vicinity of present-day South Dakota. This was a broad-headed alligatorine, which was to play a critical role in the development of subsequent North American alligators.

Three distinct species had evolved from *Alligator prenasalis* by Miocene times. The most specialized of these was undoubtedly *Alligator mcgrewi*, which has been discovered in the Marseland formation of Nebraska. It was characterized by an extremely broad head and a short snout, and attained a size of about 2 m ($6\frac{1}{2}$ ft). This species had died out by the end of the Miocene, five million years ago, and left no obvious descendants.

In contrast, *Alligator thomsoni*, which was contemporaneous with *Alligator mcgrewi* in Nebraska, appears to have continued to influence the alligator lineage down to the present day. Another broad-snouted species, it thrived in the north-west of the USA at a time when the climate in this area was much milder than it is today. From here, *Alligator thomsoni* was able to cross the land bridge in the region of the Bering Strait to reach Asia.

On this continent, it became established as the predecessor of the Chinese alligator (*Alligator sinensis*), possibly via the intermediary species known as *Alligator lucius*. Unfortunately, no adult specimen of this latter species has been discovered, but in terms of its short skull and wide jaws, there are very obvious similarities with *Alligator thomsoni*.

Meanwhile, in North America, the direct descendant of *Alligator thomsoni*, which appeared during the Pliocene in Nebraska, was *Alligator mefferdi*. This form had become isolated from the eastern population of alligators, as the Rocky Mountains formed, and created a dry area in their wake. In due course, *Alligator mefferdi* was to die out, and so this particular evolutionary line came to an end in the USA.

It was to be *Alligator olseni*, which was known to have occurred in Florida during the Miocene epoch, that led directly to the present-day American alligator (*Alligator mississippiensis*). Yet *Alligator olseni* was a relatively small species in comparison, which rarely grew beyond 2.4 m (8 ft) in overall length. Its range may have extended over a much wider area of the eastern USA but there is a lack of fossil evidence to confirm this possibility.

Traces of a subsequent Pliocene alligator have also been found in Florida. On the limited information available, it seems likely that this was indistinguishable from *Alligator mississippiensis*, which means that this species could have evolved up to five million years ago.

The remains of various alligators have been found in Europe, with the majority being characterized by the presence of the usual sockets in their upper jaw to accommodate teeth present in the lower jaw. A few, however, including *Diplocynodon*, appear to have notches rather than distinctive sockets. This was the most common genus on this continent, with a particularly long snout and a number of enlarged teeth, especially in its lower jaws. It was to be the Pleistocene Ice Age which spelt the demise of the alligatorines here.

Present-day alligatorines in South America are less evolved in some respects compared with their northern allies. Their lineage would appear to have begun during the Palaeocene epoch with the genus *Notocaiman*, whose limited remains have been found as far south as Argentina. *Eocaiman* was widely distributed across the continent in the later Eocene epoch, although an oddity in the evolutionary process in South America is raised by the discovery of a large dorsal vertebra in the Amazonas region of Brazil.

This must have come from a truly giant crocodilian, provisionally named *Dinosuchus terror*, but no other remains have been found in the intervening century since the original discovery of this monster.

Succeeding *Eocaiman* in the Oligocene epoch was a rather specialized caimanoid, christened *Balanerodus*, best known for its teeth. Its overall size remains something of a mystery, as does its lifestyle. The teeth are rather similar to acorns in appearance and suggest that *Balanerodus* was relatively large. This caimanoid may have fed on shellfish, although often its teeth are found in the company of broken mammalian bones. The possibility therefore remains that it was also a scavenger on land, if not actually an active predator.

Another rather mysterious form is *Brachygnathosuchus*, which was one of four genera believed to have occurred during Miocene times. The evidence of its existence is based on part of a right lower jaw and vertebrae obtained in Amazonas, Brazil. It appears to have had a very broad snout, with particularly long teeth at the front here. Another alligatorine genus, *Purussaurus*, is similarly known only from its snout, which appears to have been exceedingly short.

But there is more evidence to confirm the appearance of the original

Plate 59   Caimans in the past could grow to a much larger size than contemporary species, which rank amongst the smallest crocodilians.

members of the genus *Caiman*. The giant of this group was undoubtedly *Caiman neivensis*, which grew to a massive length of up to 9 m (30 ft), considerably larger than any surviving species today. Its skull alone measured 85 cm (32 in), and it hunted in the waterways of present-day Colombia.

Later caimans show a reduction in overall size, but may have ranged over a wider area than their descendants do today. *Caiman latirostris*, for example, extended south to reach Paraná in Argentina from Colombia, and could measure as much as 2.1 m (7 ft) long. This was one of the broad-snouted species.

The smallest caimans today belong to the genus *Paleosuchus*, but their fossil history is very poorly documented at present. It is known that the line had evolved by the Pliocene epoch, and subsequently, on the basis of snout size, divided into the two species now extant. Their separation from other caiman stock is thought to have taken place perhaps 30 million years ago, and since then, they have become well adapted for life in a rain-forest environment.

Very little is also known about the ancestry of the final species of caiman found in South America today, the black caiman (*Melanosuchus niger*). It is possible that this form diverged at a late stage from the main caiman line, only appearing in the fossil record as recently as the Pliocene epoch, less than five million years ago.

115

The likely ancestral form, documented from Venezuela on the basis of a couple of partial skulls, has been ascribed the scientific name of *Melanosuchus fisheri*. The snout and lower jaw are of a heavier structure, and the skull overall appears to be more robust in this case, compared with the black caiman itself.

A strange offshoot of the South American alligatorine line appeared during the Miocene epoch, although it probably played no significant part in the subsequent development of caimans in this continent. The members of the family Nettosuchidae were characterized by their long heads, with relatively few teeth present in their slender jaws. Their relationship with alligatorines tends to be confirmed by the fact that, when their jaws were closed, certain teeth at the end of the lower jaw passed in special sockets concealed in the upper jaw, as can be seen in caimans.

Even so, there is a striking similarity to members of the Stomatosuchidae family, which occurred about 70 million years previously, on the other side of the Atlantic Ocean, in Egypt. But in reality, there is no close relationship between these two specialized families, apart from the fact that they both evolved to fill a similar ecological niche.

Mourasuchus atopus, one of the better known nettosuchids, was almost certainly a passive feeder, like others of its genus. Primarily aquatic by nature, these alligatorines would have inhabited relatively still areas of water, resting with their jaws apart to catch fish which swam within reach. Possibly there may have been a soft tissue lure, as seen in some sedentary turtles today, to entice prey within its gape. Alternatively, *Mourasuchus* may have used its snout to forage for invertebrates in the mud of the pools where it lived.

The remains of this family have been found from Colombia southwards to Brazil, so it was distributed over a relatively large area. It appears that, as evolution progressed, there was a tendency for the snout of nettosuchids to become longer. But in view of their rather specialized habits, it is perhaps not surprising that this alligatorine line died out several million years ago, without leaving any obvious descendants.

THE ORIGINS OF PRESENT-DAY CROCODYLINES

Whereas the alligatorine group seems to have originated in North America and extended southwards, so the crocodyline lineage probably began in Eurasia. The crocodylines, however, spread rapidly from their Cretaceous beginnings and were soon established not only in Europe and southern Asia, but also in Africa.

Interestingly, although these reptiles were also to obtain greatest diversity at this stage in North America, they were unable to penetrate very successfully into South America, where alligatorines remained dominant. According to existing fossil remains, those that did manage to establish themselves were invaders, rather than species which had actually evolved in South America. They also tended not to compete directly with alligatorines, and differed significantly in their appearance, which was long-snouted.

One of the few crocodylines recorded in South America has been *Charactosuchus*, which was unearthed in Colombia. With its slender snout, it was almost certainly a fish-eater, and emigrated there from further north. Other earlier remains of this genus, which was also represented in the USA, have been discovered in Jamaica.

The contemporary genus *Crocodylus* was in existence by late Cretaceous times, and now accounts for nearly half of the world's 22 species of crocodilian. Only one other surviving reptilian genus has such a long ancestry. This is *Podocnemis*, which comprises a group of six species of side-necked turtle.

By the start of the Eocene epoch, *Crocodylus* species were already represented in Africa and North America. They penetrated as far south as Madagascar, where *Crocodylus robustus* survived until about one million years ago.

A number of remains of *Crocodylus* have been found in North America, much further north than surviving crocodilians. During the Eocene epoch, the climate was much milder, and so the range of *Crocodylus* was larger than it is at present. Palms were growing in southern Alaska at this stage, and the appearance of large herbivorous mammals ensured that these early crocodylines were not short of prey.

Indeed, the subfamily then comprised a greater number of genera than at any subsequent stage, with at least five having been identified from Eocene deposits in North America. Apart from *Crocodylus* and *Charactosuchus*, there was *Brachyuranochampsa*, which was a relatively large genus in terms of size, with a skull measuring 40 cm (16 in) in length. Two species have been identified in this case, showing the distinctive trait of a ridge resembling a 'V' in shape, located between the eyes. Specific changes to the pattern of dentition also characterized members of this genus.

Crocodylines of this period were relatively unspecialized, as shown by *Orthogenysuchus olseni*. This species, whose remains have been found in Wyoming, had a typical crocodilian appearance, with a broad and slightly elongated snout, and widely spaced eyes.

In North America today, the only surviving crocodyline is the American crocodile (*Crocodylus acutus*). It is not possible to trace its ancestry back to Eocene times, however, and in the absence of the fossilized evidence, it seems most likely that this species arose somewhere in the Caribbean in the relatively recent past.

Certainly, the ancestors of today's Cuban crocodile (*Crocodylus rhombifer*) appear to have ranged over a wider area in the past. Its direct ancestral form is likely to have been a species known as *Crocodylus antillensis*, although few remains of this crocodyline have been unearthed, apart from some parts of the skull.

The Orinoco crocodile (*Crocodylus intermedius*) is the most southerly representative of the genus in the New World today, extending through parts of Venezuela and Colombia in South America. But, in the past, this genus may have occurred as far south as Argentina. *Crocodylus* tends to be more temperature-sensitive than *Alligator*, however, and so, perhaps not surprisingly, it is now restricted mainly to tropical areas.

The likely ancestral form of the Nile crocodile (*Crocodylus niloticus*) is believed to be *Crocodylus lloydi*, whose remains have been discovered in Miocene rocks in Egypt. Further east, it is clear that the genus underwent a rapid expansion about five million years ago, from the start of the Pliocene epoch. In India, the fossilized appearance of *Crocodylus sivalensis* suggests that it was the predecessor of the mugger (*Crocodylus palustris*) and was also probably closely related to *Crocodylus lloydi*. Other later species, such as *Crocodylus sinhaleyus* from Sri Lanka, died out comparatively recently without leaving any direct descendants.

The occurrence of *Crocodylus* remains in Australia, such as *Crocodylus nathani*, suggest that several different crocodilians occurred simultaneously on this continent. It seems likely that some species may have colonized Australia from the break-up of the Gondwanaland supercontinent. Indeed, crocodilian remains have been uncovered in the present-day Antarctic, which is now a frozen wasteland, although in the recent past it was capable of supporting a variety of life forms. Other reptiles crossed using this land bridge, which linked South America with Australia, and there is no reason to suppose that crocodilians could not have made this journey successfully.

Much still has to be learnt about the evolution of crocodylines in the Australasian region. Scattered Pleistocene remains have been found in various localities, from Sulawesi (Celebes) to Japan. A significant number of the world's crocodylines today are still found in this area. The advent of 'genetic fingerprinting' techniques can help to unravel their interrelationships, and may give an indication of their ancestral past, in the absence of fossilized remains.

Application of these techniques to this field began in 1983, at the Louisiana State University. The results obtained tend to suggest that the surviving members of the genus *Crocodylus* are all quite closely related. While various distinct groupings can be ascertained, perhaps

Plate 60 One of the mysteries still to be resolved, in terms of the crocodilian lineage, is the evolution of the dwarf crocodile (*Osteolaemus tetraspis*).

not surprisingly the African slender-snouted crocodile (*Crocodylus cataphractus*) remains the most isolated form. The other African crocodyline, *Crocodylus niloticus*, appears to be nearest to the ancestral form of the genus and retains a general status linking it with the other members of the group.

A major advantage of this form of study is that it relies entirely on genetic material, and is not influenced by apparent physical similarities, which could misleadingly indicate a close relationship between species. As an example, although the African slender-snouted crocodile may appear noticeably similar to Johnston's crocodile (*Crocodylus johnstoni*), since both have relatively long and slender snouts, this is actually more a reflection of evolutionary pressures than evidence of a close genetic link. In reality, Johnston's crocodile is most closely related to the Orinoco crocodile (*Crocodylus intermedius*).

At the present time, the origins of the other surviving crocodyline genus in Africa, *Osteolaemus*, are unknown. This dwarf crocodile appears to have developed from more primitive stock than *Crocodylus* itself. Partly because of its small size, it superficially resembles the New World caimans. Yet, in true crocodyline fashion, it lacks the alligatorine notch in their upper jaw, and this causes the fourth tooth on each side of the lower jaw to be clearly visible. The only trace of the past of the dwarf crocodile is the discovery of sub-fossil material in Angola.

119

Chapter 6

The Crocodilian Family

In spite of the inevitable discussions over taxonomy, it is generally accepted that there are 22 distinct species of crocodilian alive at present. Out of these, however, 12 are regarded as being endangered, emphasizing the perilous status of these reptiles of ancient lineage. In some cases now, there are more individuals of a species held in captivity than are thought to exist in the wild, as in the case of the Siamese crocodile (*Crocodylus siamensis*), which is on the very verge of extinction in its native habitat.

All surviving species are discussed in this part of the book. They are classified as belonging to the order Crocodylia. The classificatory process operates via a series of ranks, down to subspecific level, where the populations concerned are clearly closely related.

Debate in the field of crocodilian taxonomy currently concerns the status of the main groups: the alligators and caimans, the crocodiles, and the gharials. The tendency in the past has been to consider these as three separate families, but more recently, they have been listed as subfamilies (Alligatorinae, Crocodylinae, Gavialinae) within the family Crocodylidae. At a lower rank, the position of the false gharial (*Tomistoma schlegelii*) is probably the most contentious. There are taxonomists who feel that it more properly belongs alongside the gharial (*Gavialis gangeticus*) itself, rather than being grouped with the crocodiles.

An example of how the classificatory system operates is given below, using the common caiman (*Caiman crocodilus*) for this purpose:

Order	Crocodylia
Family	Crocodylidae
Subfamily	Alligatorinae
Genus	*Caiman*
Species	*Caiman crocodilus*
Subspecies	*Caiman crocodilus crocodilus*
	Caiman crocodilus apaporiensis
	Caiman crocodilus fuscus
	Caiman crocodilus yacare

Only ranks from genus downwards are written in italics, which helps to establish the status of the term being used. In the case of a subspecies, in which the species' description is repeated (e.g. *Caiman crocodilus crocodilus*), this particular population is known as the nominate race. There is often doubt expressed about the validity of some subspecies, and these can vary depending on the taxonomy used. The classificatory position used here is based on that adopted by Ross (1989), with eight genera being recognized.

In order to see how this classification works out in full, there follows a full subfamily and species breakdown.

SPECIES CHECKLIST

FAMILY CROCODYLIDAE

SUBFAMILY ALLIGATORINAE: ALLIGATORS AND CAIMANS
American alligator ('gator')   *Alligator mississippiensis*
Chinese alligator   *Alligator sinensis*
Common caiman (spectacled caiman)   *Caiman crocodilus crocodilus*
    The following races are generally recognized:
    Brown caiman (American caiman)   *Caiman crocodilus fuscus*
    Apaporis River caiman   *Caiman crocodilus apaporiensis*
    Yacare caiman (red caiman)   *Caiman crocodilus yacare*
    (Two other races, *Caiman crocodilus paraguayensis* and *Caiman crocodilus matogrossiensis* have been described but are not widely considered to be valid.)
Broad-snouted caiman (broad-nosed caiman)   *Caiman latirostris*
Cuvier's smooth-fronted caiman (dwarf caiman)   *Paleosuchus palpebrosus*
Schneider's smooth-fronted caiman (Schneider's dwarf caiman)   *Paleosuchus trigonatus*

Black caiman   *Melanosuchus niger*

SUBFAMILY CROCODYLINAE: CROCODILES
American crocodile   *Crocodylus acutus*
Morelet's crocodile (Central American crocodile)   *Crocodylus moreletii*
Cuban crocodile   *Crocodylus rhombifer*
Orinoco crocodile (Colombian crocodile)   *Crocodylus intermedius*
Nile crocodile (African crocodile)   *Crocodylus niloticus*
    The following races are sometimes recognized:
    Sudanese Nile crocodile (Ethiopian Nile crocodile)   *Crocodylus niloticus niloticus*
    East African Nile crocodile   *Crocodylus niloticus africanus*

West African Nile crocodile   *Crocodylus niloticus chamses*
South African Nile crocodile   *Crocodylus niloticus corviei*
Madagascan Nile crocodile   *Crocodylus niloticus madagascariensis*
Kenyan Nile crocodile   *Crocodylus niloticus pauciscutatus*
Central African Nile crocodile   *Crocodylus niloticus suchus*
African Slender-snouted crocodile (long-nosed West African crocodile) *Crocodylus cataphractus*
Indo-Pacific crocodile (saltwater crocodile, estuarine crocodile)   *Crocodylus porosus*
Mugger (marsh crocodile)   *Crocodylus palustris*
Johnston's crocodile (Australian freshwater crocodile)   *Crocodylus johnstoni*
New Guinea crocodile   *Crocodylus novaeguineae*
Philippine crocodile (Mindoro crocodile)   *Crocodylus mindorensis*
Siamese crocodile   *Crocodylus siamensis*
Dwarf crocodile (black crocodile, broad-snouted crocodile)   *Osteolaemus tetraspis*
The following races are sometimes recognized:
West African dwarf crocodile   *Osteolaemus tetraspis tetraspis*
Congo dwarf crocodile (Osborn's dwarf crocodile)   *Osteolaemus tetraspis osborni*
False gharial (false gavial)   *Tomistoma schlegelii*

SUBFAMILY GAVIALINAE: GHARIALS
Gharial (gavial)   *Gavialis gangeticus*

Chapter 7

Alligators and Caimans

This grouping – the subfamily Alligatorinae – is comprised of seven species: two alligators and five caimans. The description 'alligator' originated from the early Spanish explorers, who visited the south-east of the USA. Here they found these large reptiles, which they soon christened *el lagarto*, meaning 'lizard'. This soon became corrupted to *aligarto* and, with further usage, the word 'alligator' evolved. Similarly, the term 'caiman' came via the Spanish, who modified it from a native Carib-Indian word.

A number of characteristic anatomical features separates this subfamily from other crocodilians. The best known is probably the arrangement of the teeth, so that the lower set are concealed in the corresponding part of the upper mouth when the jaws are closed. This is because the teeth above actually enclose those in the lower jaw at this stage. The large fourth tooth is hidden in a special hollow pit in the upper jaw, while the corresponding tooth is generally the biggest in the mouth.

Plate 61   American alligators have a significant effect on the appearance of the landscape in parts of their range, digging gator holes, which support a whole community of other creatures and plants.

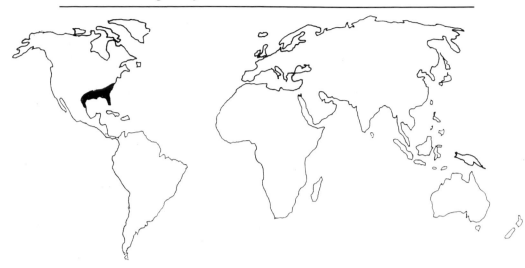

Fig. 3   Distribution of the American alligator (*Alligator mississippiensis*).

Other characteristics of the group may be less distinctive, although the snout is both broad and relatively short. Internally, the nasal bones join anteriorly with the premaxillary, and there are no sensor pits present in the ventral scales. Members of the subfamily occur exclusively in the Americas, with the notable exception of the Chinese alligator, which is found in Asia.

AMERICAN ALLIGATOR   *ALLIGATOR MISSISSIPPIENSIS*

This species is now found in only a small part of its former range. About half a million years ago, its distribution extended northwards as far as Maryland, in the south-eastern USA. Then, as the climate changed and became cooler, the alligator's habitat became smaller. The early European settlers encountered alligators in an area which extended from the far south-east of the present-day State of Virginia, westwards to the Rio Grande in Texas and in a northerly direction via the Mississippi River and its tributaries, as far as the extreme south-east of Oklahoma, north-western Mississippi and the eastern part of Arkansas. Alligators were also present throughout Florida Keys.

At this stage, much of this region was swampland, but subsequent drainage has meant that the range of the American alligator has since been greatly reduced. There was, for example, the Great Alligator Dismal Swamp in North Carolina, which extended over an area of about 2050 km² (800 sq miles). Today, although the name hints at their presence, their habitat has been dramatically changed in the interim.

Relatively large populations do still exist, however, notably in the States of Florida, Louisiana and southern Georgia. Alligators can be found in a range of habitats, including marshland, swamps, rivers, ponds and lakes. They are sometimes encountered in areas of brackish water, where the salinity does not exceed 10 parts per 1000. Unlike crocodiles, they do not possess salt glands in their mouths, but obviously their thick hides help to prevent dehydration under these conditions.

It is impossible to estimate how many alligators used to be found in the south-east of the USA, although based on the accounts of early European settlers, they were clearly common. Following heavy hunting pressures, and habitat changes, their numbers have declined, although not all human interference in the landscape was harmful for the alligators. The building of canals has made more habitat available and, in many areas within its range where more enlightened wildlife management programmes are now in force, the alligator's future seems secure. In Louisiana, as an example, the estimated population grew from just 172,000 in 1970 up to 379,000 by 1983, reflecting a growth equivalent to 120 per cent. Expansion of the alligator's range in Texas is resulting from the presence of more water holes for cattle, which can in turn be colonized by these reptiles.

Alligators play an important role in the ecology of their environment. By excavating 'gator holes', they deepen the pond concerned, ensuring a vital reservoir for other aquatic creatures as well as plants. Without the presence of an alligator, these areas would dry up quickly, like adjoining areas of water, through accumulation of silt at their base. A variety of plants thrive around the gator hole when an alligator is living there, by drawing their nourishment from the silt which has been pushed on to the bank.

As with other crocodilians, alligators are opportunist feeders. While smaller individuals take snails, amphibians, crabs and small fish, which are hunted under water, larger alligators will prey on birds, fish, snakes and mammals, including small calves. They will also hunt turtles, some of which, such as the yellow-bellied turtle (*Trachemys scripta scripta*), have evolved thicker shells than normal, in an attempt to deter such predation.

Temperature exerts a major effect on the feeding behaviour of alligators. When the water temperature falls below 20°C (68°F), alligators will usually stop feeding, with their appetite only returning as the water warms to 23°C (73°F). Studies on captive alligators have shown that a higher water temperature, between 30–32°C (86–90°F), is needed to maximize their growth potential, but if this figure rises to 39°C (102°F) it can prove fatal.

Plate 62   Alligators will take a variety of prey, but their feeding activity is noticeably affected by the environmental temperature.

Alligators today rarely exceed 4 m (13 ft) long in the case of males, while females do not normally grow beyond 2.8 m (9 ft) in length. Much larger individuals have been reported in the past, however, with a number being documented during the last century by E. A. McIlhenny. He lived on the family plantation at Avery Island, south-west Louisiana, and he and his friends could recognize the large alligators which lived in the vicinity. The biggest, which they had christened 'Old Monsurat' was shot in the autumn of 1879, and four mules were needed to drag the carcass out of the water. It measured 5.6 m (18¼ ft) overall.

Other slightly smaller individuals were also recorded by McIlhenny, but he himself killed the longest alligator ever known. He saw it on a cold January morning during 1890, lying inert in a marsh. It was not possible to bring it on to solid ground, but in terms of length, it measured 5.6 m (19 ft 2 in). Its teeth were virtually worn away, and McIlhenny was convinced that this aged giant was already on the point of death when he came across it.

In Florida, the largest alligator on record is one that was shot at Lake Apopka during 1956. This individual was 5.3 m (17 ft 5 in) overall, and appeared quite active. But an even larger specimen probably originated from the vicinity of the Sebastian River in 1886. Unfortunately, it is known only from the remains of its skull, but it has been suggested

Plates 63 and 64   Young alligators (above) are relatively colourful compared with adults (below), usually having a number of yellow stripes on their bodies.

that this particular alligator was over 5.5 m (18 ft) in length.

American alligators do vary somewhat in body shape, with some being slimmer than others. This may be related to their lifestyles. In Louisiana, females tend to occupy more remote areas, close to vegetation, whereas males often congregate in stretches of open water. Here they may have a more active way of life. Certainly it is clear from

127

observations on captive individuals that their heads are often wider than those of their wild counterparts, possibly because they spend less time swimming in water, and rest for longer periods on land.

Female alligators are mound-builders, and lay clutches of between 20 and 50 eggs. These start to hatch about 65 days later. Other animals may take advantage of the security provided by this nest site, notably the Florida red-bellied turtle (*Pseudemys nelsoni*). As many as 200 turtle eggs have been found in association with a single alligator nest, and it appears that the young chelonians can survive in the company of hatchling alligators, although presumably some may be eaten.

Young alligators are more brightly coloured than adults, being black with a number of yellow bands across their body and tail. These bands generally fade as they grow older, but may provide some disruptive camouflage during the early stages of life. Adults, equipped with about 40 teeth in their jaws, are greenish black above, enabling them to conceal themselves very effectively in areas of sluggish water, especially where there is vegetation on the surface. Their underparts are paler, being yellowish, and osteoderms may be present on their ventral surface, depending on the population concerned.

There is said to be a difference in coloration noticeable between juveniles from the western part of their present range and those found further eastwards, from Mississippi through to Florida. White speckling is present in the vicinity of the jaws of the western group, and their stripes are also somewhat paler.

It has been suggested that this difference has arisen from the effects of

Fig. 4   Distribution of the Chinese alligator (*Alligator sinensis*).

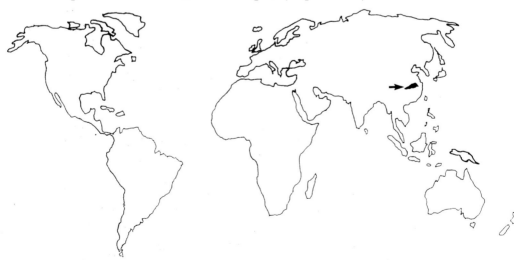

the decline in temperature during the Pleistocene epoch, about half a million years ago. At this stage, as the ice sheets spread down from the north, so the average temperature in this part of the USA would have declined, forcing the alligator to retreat into two refuges.

The western population remained confined to the Mississippi delta, with the eastern distribution of the species being restricted to the relatively mild area of the Florida peninsula. It is clear even today that the average annual minimum temperature is a major determining influence on the alligator's distribution in the USA. Alligators are only found south of the $-9.4°C$ (15°F) isotherm.

During the intervening years, as the ice sheets retreated in the far north and the area began to warm up, so the two populations appear to have reunited. They were not separated for a sufficiently long period to have evolved into subspecies. Indeed no difference is discernible in the appearance of adults, although juveniles in the eastern part of the range tend to lose their pattern of markings at a somewhat earlier stage than those occurring further west.

CHINESE ALLIGATOR   *ALLIGATOR SINENSIS*

This species remained essentially undocumented in the West until it was seen in Shanghai by the zoologist Robert Swinhoe, who travelled widely in this part of the world. He saw one being displayed in a pit here during February 1869. It measured about 1.2 m (4 ft) in length, and apparently had been caught in the Province of Shensi. Although Swinhoe tried to buy it, its captors refused, because so many people were paying to view the reptile.

The range of the Chinese alligator has contracted sharply during recent centuries. From Swinhoe's account, it is clear that, by this stage, these crocodilians were already largely unknown to the people in the area of Shanghai. In Chinese records, the first reference apparently relating to the alligator here dates back to the third century A.D. It is linked with the mythical dragon, under the names *tou lung* and *yow lung*.

Later, the explorer Marco Polo described what was clearly a crocodilian, which reputedly occurred in part of the province known today as Yunnan. He related how these reptiles were hunted using sharp spikes hidden in the ground along the paths which they used. As an alligator walked over the spikes, so they brutally ripped open its belly. The gall bladder was the major prize from the kill and was used to treat various ailments, from rabies (for which purpose it was administered in wine) to carbuncles. It was in demand as an analgesic for use during labour, and the alligator's flesh was also highly valued.

According to a priest who visited China during 1656, these alligators

129

were then quite common in the Jinsha Jiang, better known as the Yangtze River. Their range used to extend westwards along the Yangtze into Hubei Province, where the species could be found in the Yunmeng swamps. It was also present in Hunan Province, and occurred further northwards than today, in Huang He, which is also known as the Yellow River.

Reports of the occurrence of this species in Korea, based solely on literature, are unlikely to be accurate. Not only is the climate here unfavourable, with the winters being even colder than in the USA, but the rivers are generally fast-flowing and shallow. Such habitat is not ideally suited to these crocodilians, since they tend to be found in rather sluggish stretches of water, which includes lakes and pools.

The present distribution of the Chinese alligator appears to be restricted to the Provinces of Anhui, Zhejang and Jiangsu in the lower part of the Yangtze valley. It is a small species, according to the specimens in collections today, which rarely exceeds 2 m ($6\frac{1}{2}$ ft) in overall length, although individuals up to 3 m (10 ft) have been recorded in the past.

Through the winter, these alligators retreat into burrows. These may be relatively expansive areas, dug in the soft, sandy soil. They can extend to a depth of 3 m (10 ft), and, here, the temperature is unlikely to fall below 10°C (50°F). It seems likely that the alligators do not feed for the bulk of this time, and start to emerge from their burrows again around the middle of April.

Mating takes place during June, with both males and females bellowing at this stage. In true crocodilian fashion, the male then twists his tail slightly under that of the female, in order to achieve penetration. The penis, which is bent in shape, is forced from the cloaca where it is usually retained, out into the female's cloaca. The semen is transferred from the vas deferens via a simple channel, leading from this opening to the base of the organ.

Egg-laying follows from mid-July through until August, with each female preparing a mound comprised mainly of leaves and grasses. Here they will ultimately deposit between 10 and 50 eggs, each weighing about 45 g ($1\frac{1}{2}$ oz) and measuring around 6 cm (2 in) in length. The incubation period lasts approximately 70 days, with the hatchlings averaging 21 cm (8 in) long when they emerge from their eggs and weighing in at about 30 g (1 oz). They are black in colour, with yellow stripes on their bodies, and can climb easily as well as swim at this stage.

Growth is rapid, with the young alligators eating a variety of aquatic snails, which comprise the major item of their diet, as well as fish and freshwater mussels. They will be mature by about four years of age, but are especially at risk from the effects of winter floods. Large numbers of

Chinese alligators were drowned in their burrows as a consequence of flooding during 1957, and there is also increasing human encroachment on their habitat.

The present population of this species may not exceed 300 individuals in total, occupying a total area of about 25,000 km^2 (9650 sq miles). Faced with increasing isolation, the threat to these alligators is becoming greater. If they are forced to journey overland in a bid to find a mate, they may then be killed by the local people. Thankfully, however, the presence of osteoderms in their belly hide has meant that these alligators have not been persecuted for the skin trade.

Attempts are being made by the Chinese government to conserve this species. A rearing unit, which will also purchase adults caught by the local people, was set up at Xuancheng, in Anhui Province. Shanghai Zoo has also been successful in breeding this species, while outside the People's Republic of China, stock is established at the Rockefeller Wildlife Refuge in Louisiana, USA.

The original three adult Chinese crocodiles used in this particular project were all believed to be over 40 years old at the outset, and originated from zoos within the USA. Since then, further adults have been obtained from collections in the Federal Republic of Germany and Hungary. Breeding began during 1977, with a second colony then being founded at Houston Zoo in Texas.

In spite of its perceived fearsome reputation, the Chinese alligator is actually a shy and rather retiring species. It is not dangerous to people. Field studies are presently being carried out throughout its native range to gain a more detailed insight into the effective measures that must be taken to ensure its survival here.

COMMON CAIMAN   *CAIMAN CROCODILUS*

There is considerable dispute over the taxonomy of this species. Most herpetologists accept that four different subspecies occur through its wide range, across much of Central and South America. Its area of distribution extends from southern Mexico southwards as far as northern parts of Argentina, and it has also been introduced to some localities in Florida in the USA.

Common caimans are relatively small and highly adaptable crocodilians. They rarely grow to 2.5 m (8 ft) in length, although a few individuals over 3 m (10 ft) have been recorded. Huge numbers can be present in some areas, especially where they are protected. In Venezuela, for example, it is estimated that there are four million common caimans, and the permitted hunting quota of 150,000 per

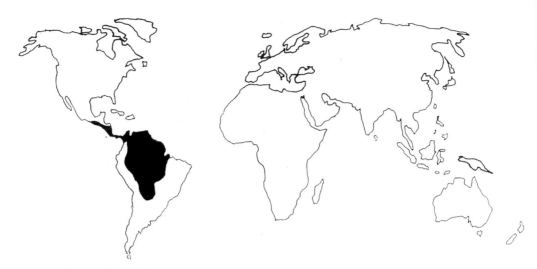

Fig. 5   Distribution of the common caiman (*Caiman crocodilus*).

annum could possibly double, depending on field studies, over the next few years, without any adverse effects on the overall population here. Both ranchers and tanners in Venezuela contribute 50 cents per skin to fund independent monitoring of caiman numbers in the wild.

Population declines have occurred in some other countries, such as Peru, because of unregulated trade. It is clear, however, that provided hunting pressures can be curtailed effectively, the status of the species will improve before long, assuming the habitat is unaffected. Common caimans are most likely to be encountered in areas of relatively still water, ranging from marshland to lakes and slow-flowing rivers. Youngsters feed mainly on aquatic invertebrates, but adults will also take larger prey, including wild pigs.

In some areas during the dry season, pools dry up, and then the caimans will congregate in remaining stretches of water. They can survive in brackish surroundings. On occasions, caimans will burrow into the mud at the bottom of a pool which has virtually dried up, aestivating until the return of the rains.

In Venezuela, the flooded areas of savanna, known as the llanos, are susceptible to drying up, and at this stage, the caimans generally cease to feed, although some observations suggest that cannibalism increases during this period. The availability of more permanent areas of water here, because of reservoirs built for cattle, has assisted them in maintaining their numbers.

Mating usually takes place right at the end of the dry season, with egg-laying occurring as the water levels start to rise again. This helps to ensure a good supply of food for the young caimans when they hatch, which is within a period of three months.

Communal nesting is often a feature with this species, and may have strategic survival significance. Females construct a broad-based mound of suitable vegetation, where they lay up to 40 eggs. The main nest predators are likely to be the large tegu lizards (*Tupinambis* species), which may outwit the attempts of the female caiman to protect her nest. Predation can be high, with over 80 per cent of nests being destroyed in some areas.

Young caimans, usually hatched around November in northern South America, initially remain together in groups, overseen by females. On emerging from their eggs, they are about 15 cm (6 in) in length. They mature quickly, and may breed for the first time when only four years old. Hatchlings are yellowish marked with black spots and bands, but this coloration alters later in life, with the body of adults being a dull shade of olive-green.

A distinctive feature of this species is its apparent ability to change colour, especially if it becomes cold. Known as metachrosis, this results from an expansion of the black pigment cells, called melanophores. Interestingly, the southerly races assume a similar appearance to that of the Central American subspecies, known as the brown caiman (*Caiman crocodilus fuscus*), which, as its name suggests, is a dusky shade of olive-brown in the more northerly parts of the species' range. Those found in South America tend to show greater similarity to the nominate race.

The brown caiman is slightly smaller, growing to a maximum length of about 1.8 m (6 ft). It has become scarce in various parts of its range because of excessive hunting, and large numbers of hatchlings used to be captured for the pet trade. In areas of water where the caiman population has declined, the overall ecosystem often suffers and there follows a noticeable fall in the number of fish.

This is because the caimans contribute valuable nutrients to the water via their excrement, which is broken down via the nitrogen cycle, and in turn nourishes a variety of plants and invertebrate life. Without this vital source of nutrients, there is less food available in the food chain, and this is manifested by a declining fish population.

The most restricted of the recognized races of the common caiman is the Rio Apaporis race (*Caiman crocodilus apaporiensis*), which is confined to a 200-km (125-mile) length of this river, located in the south-east of Colombia. It was first described during 1955, and plans are in progress to ensure its survival, with the establishment of captive breeding groups. One of the main features of this race is its remarkably narrow snout, and it is also more colourful than the nominate race.

Plate 65   The common caiman (*Caiman crocodilus*) is one of the most widely distributed of all crocodilians. Note the spectacles around the eyes, which have given rise to the alternative name for this species, the spectacled caiman.

The southernmost subspecies has become endangered because of excessive hunting. The Yacare caiman (*Caiman crocodilus yacare*) has suffered badly from a lack of enforcement of existing protective legislation. It is hunted for the leather trade in spite of the presence of osteoderms on the skin of its belly. Yacare caimans are often encountered in association with floating mats of vegetation, some of which is sometimes found in their stomachs, having been accidentally ingested. Aquatic snails again appear to form a significant part of their diet, as well as crabs and occasionally snakes.

The pattern of dentition of the Yacare caiman differs somewhat from members of other races, because larger teeth present in the lower jaw may actually pass right through the upper jaw and protrude on the surface of the snout. As with other subspecies, so-called 'spectacles', formed by ridges surrounding and extending in front of the eye, are clearly evident.

An interesting experiment carried out with common caimans shed some light on the function of the scent glands in the mouth. A dummy was used to encourage a mature female to display breeding behaviour. As part of this response, the gland became visible and, possibly, its secretions may help to stimulate a mating response from the male.

BROAD-SNOUTED CAIMAN   *CAIMAN LATIROSTRIS*

Present in a wide area of eastern and south-eastern South America, away from the Amazon basin, this caiman occurs in parts of Brazil, Argentina, Uruguay, Bolivia and Paraguay. It can be distinguished by its broad head, and the presence of a ridge running down the snout. The overall length of the broad-snouted caiman rarely exceeds 3 m (10 ft), with most individuals being around 2 m ($6\frac{1}{2}$ ft long). Its body coloration is dark greenish, with blotches on the jaw, so that at first glance, it could be confused with the Yacare caiman (*Caiman crocodilus yacare*).

The habitat of the broad-snouted caiman includes mangrove swamps and other areas of brackish water. It prefers stretches of water where there is good plant cover, and is by nature a highly aquatic species. Being found further south than most other caimans, it is apparently less sensitive to cold than species found nearer the equator. The dark body coloration of both the broad-snouted caiman and the Yacare caiman doubtless helps them to absorb the heat of the sun by radiation. It conserves the available warmth from the environment in

Fig. 6   Distribution of the broad-snouted caiman (*Caiman latirostris*).

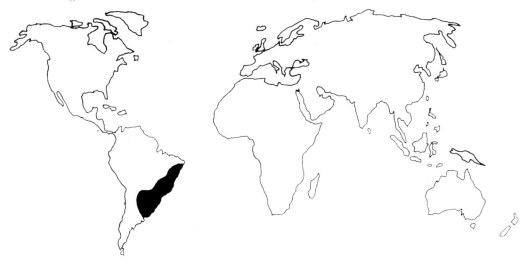

135

their bodies as effectively as possible. They tend to bask for relatively short periods, even during the summer, and may only leave the water on sunny days in the winter time, when the ambient air temperature is lower.

Broad-snouted caimans are very shy and secretive by nature, often preferring to hunt at night. They feed on a range of aquatic invertebrates, including snails, and crustaceans such as crabs. Bigger prey, notably mammals and birds, will be taken by larger individuals. Their broad jaws may also be used to crush the shells of turtles.

Breeding takes place in the period from August to March, beginning earlier in the northern part of the range. Females will often retreat to islands in the rivers, where they bask and construct their nests. A typical nest for this species measures about 1.6 m (5 ft) across and is about 40 cm (16 in) in height. The eggs are laid in two tiers, separated by a layer of nesting material. The local temperature differential created by this arrangement may help to ensure that both sexes are represented amongst the hatchlings (see page 92).

The number of eggs laid typically ranges from 20 to 60, each being approximately 7 cm ($2\frac{1}{2}$ in) long and weighing 84 g (3 oz). In some cases, the male caiman has been known to assist with nest-building, and he is subsequently involved in watching over the hatchlings once they emerge from the eggs. Females remain near to the nest throughout the incubation period, which lasts about ten weeks. They will then break open the nest and carry their offspring to water.

The belly skin of the broad-snouted caiman has been much in demand by the leather trade, and populations have been brought to the verge of extinction in some areas. The scales on the underparts are relatively even in size, and considered ideal for the manufacture of top-quality leather products. In contrast to skins obtained from the common caiman, the resulting leather is extremely supple after tanning because it is relatively free from osteoderms. Interestingly, although their ranges overlap to some extent, they tend not to be found in the same localities.

In all countries where it occurs, the broad-snouted caiman is declining, through inadequate protection, although other factors, such as pollution of waterways, can also be cited in this respect. The effluent from Pôrto Alegre in Brazil, for example, is threatening the survival of the species in the Los Patos Lake, while elsewhere in Brazil, habitat modification is also having a detrimental effect on its numbers. Drainage projects are a particular problem for the existing population in Uruguay, although its range here has been increased recently, to include Laguna Negra and part of Laguna Merim.

The result of the disappearance of this caiman from many of its former haunts has seen an apparent corresponding incidence of fluke infections of cattle and people. This may be linked to the fact that broad-snouted caimans feed extensively on aquatic snails, which are known to be an intermediate host of this parasite.

It has been suggested that there are two subspecies of the broad-snouted caiman, although this view is not universally accepted. The larger nominate race is generally the more adaptable form, with the subspecies *Caiman latirostris chacoensis* being significantly smaller, rarely exceeding 1.8 m (6 ft) in length, and confined to parts of Argentina.

BLACK CAIMAN *MELANOSUCHUS NIGER*

Another species which has been heavily persecuted for its skin, the black caiman is also the largest of the South American crocodilians. It can grow to over 6 m (20 ft) long and, despite a superficial resemblance to the American alligator, it is definitely a caiman, although it differs from members of the genus *Caiman* in several significant respects. The orbit, where the eyeball is located, is much larger and, anatomically, the skull structure is unorthodox, with the vomer component being clearly evident on the palate. Although the snout itself is quite wide at its base, it rapidly becomes rather narrow and pointed in a rostral direction. Nevertheless, as in the case of the other two caiman genera, the clear bony ridge present above the orbit, extending down the snout from above the eyes, is still clearly evident.

Its area of distribution is centred on the Amazon drainage basin, but

Fig. 7   Distribution of the black caiman (*Melanosuchus niger*).

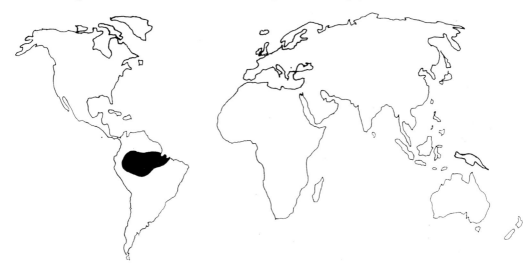

Plate 66 The black caiman (*Melanosuchus niger*), an attractive species which has declined significantly in numbers because of hunting pressure. Larger individuals have occasionally been reported to attack people, but generally caimans are inoffensive.

it does extend further north also, into south-western Guyana for example, where black caimans are known to occur on the Rupununi River. Although recorded in the north-east of Peru and Bolivia, it seems unlikely that the species ranges as far south as Paraguay, in spite of some reports. For reasons which are unclear, it has also never been present in Surinam.

Today, the largest populations probably remain in French Guiana, and here also, the biggest individuals can be found, in the vicinity of Kaw. But overall, it has been estimated that, within the space of little more than a century, the overall population has declined by 99 per cent through its range.

These caimans inhabit areas of shallow water, often venturing into flooded areas of forest close to lakes or smaller ponds. In more conspicuous localities, such as the Amazon River itself, they have almost totally disappeared. In some ways, the actions of the black caiman are rather suggestive of a terrestrial ancestry. It tends to hunt by sight and

138

sound, lunging forward at prey, which is seized precisely by the tip of its snout in the shallows. The hearing ability of this species is especially acute.

Juvenile black caimans, like related crocodilians, hunt for crustaceans and other invertebrates, including snails, as well as feeding on fish. Adults tend to feed more on large rodents, such as the capybara (*Hydrochaeris hydrochaeris*), turtles and deer, although the major part of their diet appears to be comprised of fish. Various catfishes, as well as piranhas, are favoured prey. On occasions, they may resort to domesticated animals, including dogs and pigs, and can occasionally attack people as well.

Black caimans tend to hunt at night and, during the dry season, prey is readily available. As the water level shrinks, so fish are forced to congregate in shallow pools. Here, in the lower reaches of the Amazon basin, they are easily accessible to the caimans during late December each year. Females start nesting about this time, depending on the locality. They build a nest of plant material, which can average 1.5 m (5 ft) in diameter and up to 80 cm ($2\frac{1}{2}$ ft) in height.

It takes about six weeks for the embryos to develop to the point of hatching. The clutch size is generally quite large, numbering as many as 65 eggs, although 50 to 60 is probably average. Only in some localities will the female appear to defend the nest site. While some nests are well concealed in a forest setting, others are sited in a more open locality. Lying across her nest in the latter areas, the female will absorb heat both from the ground and the sun.

Such behaviour may help also to stabilize the temperature inside the nest mound. In some cases, a number of females may have built within a relatively small locality, so potentially there will be a large number of hatchlings within a confined area. As a reproductive strategy, this means that a significant number should survive.

Hunting of the black caiman began in earnest during the 1940s, and, even as recently as the early 1970s, around 66,000 hides were being exported annually from Colombia. Here today, as a direct result of this unregulated pressure, the species is virtually extinct. During a two-month survey carried out in 1977, in the vicinity of the Colombian Amazon and Putumayo Rivers, none was sighted in the wild. A problem affecting the revival of this species is its occurrence alongside the more adaptable common caiman. This latter species is a much shyer crocodilian, and harder to catch as a result, although more common. It has benefited from the decline of its larger relative, moving into areas of its former habitat and spreading beyond, to new man-made localities. The common caiman can reproduce more quickly and so its widespread presence encourages hunting activity through its range.

Unfortunately, the hunters themselves are less selective, and so in areas where the species occur together, the remaining black caimans are relatively easy to take, with the hunting pressure being maintained. Once their heads have been removed, it is difficult to distinguish between the two species, and so trade in the skins of the endangered black caiman can continue almost unchecked.

Much of its range falls outside present national park boundaries, and increasing development still threatens its present strongholds, as at Kaw. The practice of burning the swampland here during the dry period also represents a danger to these caimans, as they may be unable to escape the flames. Up to 1000 breeding black caimans may be present in this region, so it is a considerable factor in their survival. A similarly valuable group occurs within the Manu National Park in Peru, where their protection is probably more assured.

In areas where black caimans have declined noticeably in numbers, clear effects of this loss can be seen on the environment. The resulting growth in capybara populations in Brazil and Bolivia has led to serious agricultural losses, since the numbers of these rodents are no longer curbed effectively by the caimans. Cattle are also reputed to be attacked more frequently by the notorious piranha (*Serrasalmus piraya*) in areas of flooded pasture, where caimans formerly used to catch such fish.

The effects on the food chain have been equally significant, since with less organic matter from the caimans' excrement in certain stretches of water, there is less food available for fish fry. It has been followed by a shortage of economically important fish in areas where they were previously common, alongside the black caiman.

In the case of the black caiman, hatchlings do not alter significantly in appearance as they grow older. They are black along the back, with very pale yellow bands of dots on the sides of the body, extending back from the base of the head. These bands are still evident in adults, although they may become more whitish in later life. The head itself is a lightish shade of grey, with darker bands extending down across the jaws.

CUVIER'S DWARF CAIMAN *PALEOSUCHUS PALPEBROSUS*

The generic description *Paleosuchus* translates as 'ancient crocodile', and reflects the view that the two members of this genus are the relics of an old line which evolved from the traditional caiman group at least 30 million years ago. Anatomically, they lack the ridges on the head which are associated with other species, although the front of the skull is well

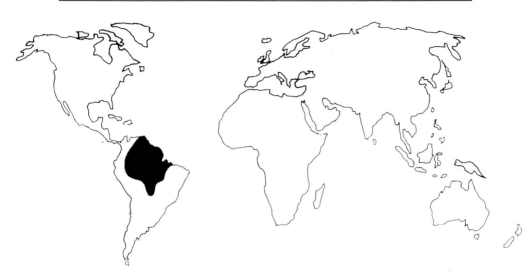

Fig. 8   Distribution of Cuvier's dwarf caiman (*Paleosuchus palpebrosus*).

protected by bone, with the upper eyelids also having a component of bone in them.

In fact, these caimans have more heavily ossified dermal armour than any other crocodilians. This may be a reflection partly of their small size, which would otherwise leave them more vulnerable to predators. In addition, this armour helps to prevent injury from sharp rocks and other projections in the fast-flowing waters where they may be found.

The structure of their skull is also very different from that of other crocodilians, being not unlike that of a dog. The snout itself is quite short, while the overall shape of the head is not flattened, but raised and smooth. This relative lack of streamlining may simply reflect the fact that this species is not highly aquatic by nature. Indeed, it is known to spend time in burrows during the day, and it may range quite widely on land. Certainly, these dwarf caimans are often encountered in areas of flooded forest, but rarely in more open stretches of water, or streams running through the rainforest.

Cuvier's dwarf caiman is the smallest of the New World crocodilians, with males growing to a maximum size of 1.5 m (5 ft). Females are smaller, not exceeding 1.2 m (4 ft) overall. In spite of their size, however, these caimans appear tolerant of low temperatures. One which escaped from the Institute of National Sciences in Bogotá, Colombia, was rediscovered in a pool nearby, feeding on frogs, although the water temperature here at night could fall to a minimum of 6°C (43°F).

These caimans do not occur in large numbers in any locality, and

141

seem to have a rather solitary lifestyle. This may be a reflection of a relative shortage of suitable prey, especially in fast-flowing stretches of water. Cuvier's dwarf caiman has teeth which are sharp and curve backwards in the mouth. These probably assist in grabbing fishes and other creatures in such surroundings, although their feeding habits are not well known. It seems clear that they do take a variety of aquatic invertebrates as well, including freshwater shrimps and crabs, plus amphibians, rodents, birds, snakes and possibly smaller caiman. Being so widely distributed across much of northern South America, their diet almost certainly varies somewhat according to the locality.

Very little has been observed about their breeding habits in the wild, although the female will amass a mound of material, incorporating leaves, grass and other vegetation. Mud will be added to help to bind the structure together. It is usually located in a concealed position, largely but not entirely hidden from the sun. At the core of the nest mound, the female will deposit her clutch of up to 25 eggs in a muddy hollow, before finally sealing the chamber. They are each about 7 cm (3 in) long and take about three months to hatch.

It is presumed that she remains nearby through this period, and digs the youngsters out of the cavity when they start calling. By this stage, the mud is likely to have hardened into a fairly impenetrable barrier for the young caimans. Subsequently, however, it appears that she has no interest in her offspring, and there is evidence that some may be cannibalized.

Young Cuvier's dwarf caimans have a yellowish brown area on their

Fig. 9   Distribution of Schneider's dwarf caiman (*Paleosuchus trigonatus*).

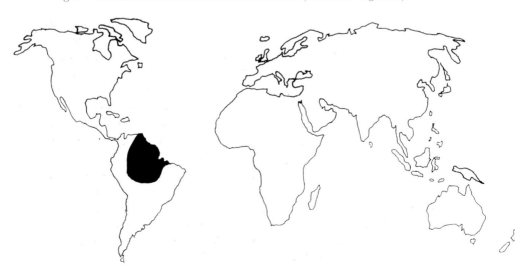

heads, which will darken to the rusty shade of adults by the time they are about six months old. The body is banded by darker lines in hatchlings, which provide valuable camouflage. It will be a day or so following their emergence from the egg before the young caimans head for water. Their bodies are coated with slime, and this apparently dries before they immerse themselves for the first time.

The slime may have some protective function, guarding against infections. Certainly, an interesting characteristic of Cuvier's dwarf caiman is its susceptibility to the growth of filamentous algae on its body. Under normal circumstances, this appears to cause the reptile no harm and provides additional camouflage but, in some cases, especially with ailing caimans, the algal growth reaches severe proportions.

The status of this species is unclear, but in view of its distribution, second only to that of the common caiman in South America, it is not endangered. In addition, the bony body covering extends to the ventral surface, and the osteoderms here are very extensive, rendering the species of no value for its hide. As a result, it has escaped the drastic effects of human predation, although it may be hunted locally by Indians as a source of food.

SCHNEIDER'S DWARF CAIMAN *PALEOSUCHUS TRIGONATUS*

The *Paleosuchus* caimans are also sometimes described as smooth-fronted caimans, because they lack the ridge present between the eyes of other genera. Schneider's dwarf caiman is somewhat larger in size than its relative. Males generally grow up to 1.7 m ($5\frac{1}{2}$ ft), with females reaching 1.4 m ($4\frac{1}{2}$ ft) overall.

The distribution of the two species of dwarf caiman overlaps to a considerable extent. They range through the Amazon and Orinoco basins, with Schneider's dwarf caiman being found from the Guianas and Venezuela in a southerly direction as far as the State of Bahia in Brazil. Cuvier's dwarf caiman extends somewhat further south from this point, which suggests that it may be more tolerant of cold conditions. The relationship between these two species in the wild is unclear. It has been suggested that, since Schneider's dwarf caiman has a more pointed snout, it may be found in fast-flowing stretches of water, since this feature would lessen water resistance. It is again well protected, with large and sharp scutes covering the neck and tail. These are more prominent than in Cuvier's dwarf caiman. The tail is especially shielded, having little flexibility as a result, with the double row of scutes here being relatively large, and protruding laterally as well, which effectively increases its width.

These dwarf caimans are rarely seen basking, although they will venture on to land at night. Radio-tracking has shown that they may cover considerable distances, perhaps searching for prey. They walk with their necks raised, and their short tails prove advantageous to moving over land.

Schneider's dwarf caiman inhabits rain-forest streams, which are often quite shallow, so that part of the body remains exposed above the water's surface. Adults tend to live separate lives, establishing territories which can extend as far as 1000 m (1100 yd) along a suitable stretch of water. They appear less dependent on their aquatic environment for food than other crocodilians, however, with even juveniles hunting birds, rodents and similar small mammals out of water. Fish forms only a relatively minor part of their diet, but proportionately more reptiles, such as snakes and lizards, are probably taken.

Breeding activity occurs at the end of the dry season throughout the range of these caimans, with the female constructing a nest which may be located close to a termite's mound. This helps to provide additional heat to assist the incubation process. Clutch size is generally quite small, rarely exceeding 15 eggs, and the hatchlings emerge as the rains are swelling the streams, which may enhance their chances for survival.

As with Cuvier's dwarf caiman, the belly skin is comprised of osteoderms which overlap, ensuring that this species is of no value in the leather trade. It may actually prove to be common through its range, although its present population status is unclear. Few animals prey on these caimans when they are adult, with the notable exception of anacondas. One such snake, measuring about 5.9 m (19$\frac{1}{2}$ ft) managed to swallow a Schneider's dwarf caiman which was itself 1.8 m (6 ft) in length. In spite of its bony casing, the caiman was being effectively consumed by the snake. Its digestive juices had started to break down the crocodilian's skin at the time of its own death. The dark body coloration of the caiman had been most noticeably affected by this stage, rendering it much paler than in life.

Chapter 8

Crocodiles

Today, 13 species of crocodile – the sub-family Crocodylinae – still occur in the world, confined largely to tropical areas. They tend to be somewhat similar in appearance, with snouts which are reasonably broad, narrowing towards the tip in most cases. In terms of dentition, the feature which distinguishes them from the alligators and caimans is the arrangement of the fourth tooth relative to the upper jaw.

Although the rest of the teeth fit into pits, this particular tooth on each side of the face actually slides into a notch, and remains apparent even when the jaws are closed, since all crocodilians lack lips. There are also sensory areas on the ventral scale, and salt glands, which are especially prominent in the case of the Indo-Pacific crocodile (*Crocodylus porosus*).

AMERICAN CROCODILE   *CROCODYLUS ACUTUS*

This species is the most widely distributed of the four crocodiles present in the New World. A small population occurs in the southern part of Florida, being found here mainly in the Keys and the Everglades. Its mainland distribution then extends from Mexico, via Belize and other Central American countries, into Colombia and Venezuela in South

Fig. 10   Distribution of the American crocodile (*Crocodylus acutus*).

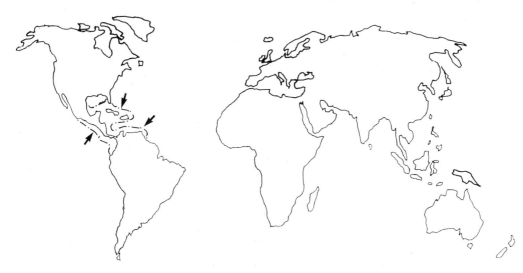

145

Plate 67   The distinctive feature of a crocodile, the presence of the fourth tooth protruding above the level of the upper jaw, rather than being concealed, is clearly demonstrated here.

America. On the western side of this continent, its range extends through the coastal zone of Ecuador as far as the Rio Chira in Peru. American crocodiles have also successfully colonized many islands in the Caribbean, with the species being represented here on Cuba, Jamaica, Hispaniola, Trinidad, Margarita and several of the Cayman Islands. Off the Pacific coast of Mexico, the species is present on the Tres Marias Islands as well.

Large individuals can measure up to 7 m $(21\frac{1}{2}$ ft$)$ in length, with males again being bigger than females. Today, however, American crocodiles over 4 m (13 ft) are a rarity. They can be distinguished by the dramatic reduction in the osteoderms on their dorsal surface, fewer than any other crocodilian. There is also an obvious swelling present on the snout of both mature and juvenile individuals in front of the eye sockets, although this feature is not obvious in hatchlings, which tend to be more colourful. While adult American crocodiles are often of an

Plate 68   A species at home both in the sea and in fresh water, the American crocodile (*Crocodylus acutus*) is widely distributed throughout the Caribbean.

olive-brown shade, youngsters are much lighter, with darker banding on their bodies, including the tail.

This species tends to occur primarily in coastal areas, frequenting both brackish and freshwater localities, and sometimes spreading further inland up river systems. They may colonize areas of water introduced by human activity, notably in Florida, where canals cut through mangrove swamps offer a secure habitat and suitable peat banks which can be used as nesting sites.

Adult American crocodiles are more suited to survive in areas of salty water than hatchlings. Indeed, on some small islands in the Caribbean, they live without access to fresh water. Larger individuals are better able to withstand hypersaline conditions compared with hatchlings, because they have a smaller surface area to volume ratio. Although there is a salt gland in the mouth, as with all crocodiles, this does not appear to function as an effective osmoregulatory organ. Instead, the crocodiles take advantage of fresh water in the environment, following rainfall for example, and drink to maintain their fluid balance.

The American crocodile is known to excavate burrows through most of its range. These can be quite complex, with more than one entrance. One such tunnel reported on the Rio Palenque in Colombia had a

147

point of entry above water and measured 2.75 m ($7\frac{1}{2}$ ft) long, while another, in the form of a subterranean tunnel, was nearly 6 m ($18\frac{1}{2}$ ft) in length. At the rear, there was a big chamber, measuring about 7.2×8.5 m^2 (20×23 ft^2) in size. Burrows of this type provide a retreat against predators, and can be used for aestivation when the nearby water levels fall to a critically low level for the crocodilians.

American crocodiles are most likely to be seen on land during the early morning or late afternoon, when they emerge from the water or their burrows to raise their body temperature under the sun's rays. When the weather is warm, the crocodiles tend to retreat to deeper areas of water, although at night they may occasionally be encountered on land. This is often linked to high wind speeds, whipping the water into waves which may make breathing more difficult for the crocodiles.

Out of water, American crocodiles may display the typical mouth-gaping seen in other species as well. Various explanations have been put forward to explain such behaviour. Perhaps the most obvious is that this action may have a thermo-regulatory basis. But allowing the lining of the mouth to become dry could also help to limit the risk of fungal infections developing here. It could also be a means of preventing algal growth, which might otherwise prove disruptive to the development of new teeth for example.

While young crocodiles feed on both aquatic and terrestrial vertebrates, as well as small fish, it is this latter item which is most significant in the diet of adults. They may congregate in relatively shallow areas, hunting both *Tilapia* and *Cichlasoma*. One observer has suggested that American crocodiles have an active means of attracting such food to them. They regurgitate a very small quantity of food, via the gullet, into the mouth. Fish will soon be attracted in some numbers, making them much easier to catch as a result.

Turtles also feature prominently in the diet of some of these crocodiles, with their hard shells being cracked quite easily in the crocodilian's jaw. The crocodiles often hunt at night, and are sometimes blamed, with justification, for the disappearance of domestic animals, including dogs and goats. Although this species is said to be a threat to people, it appears that, in reality, attacks are very few in numbers.

Females are mature by the time they are 2.5 m (7 ft) long. After mating, they will search out a suitable nesting site, which may have been used during previous years. They emerge on to land here at night, and dig the nesting hole with their hind legs. Only in parts of Florida does this species construct a nesting mound.

Studies of the Mexican population show that hatchlings stay together in pods, supervised by the female for several weeks. But this may be exceptional – certainly young American crocodiles vocalize less than most other species, which suggests that they tend to separate at an early stage in life.

It has been suggested, however, that hunting of this species may have altered maternal behaviour. Crocodilians undoubtedly have a learning ability and, where populations are heavily predated, it is clear that groups would be more vulnerable than individuals. Historical accounts dating back to the seventeenth century suggest that American crocodiles then retained more interest in their hatchlings than they do today.

Studies of nesting sites of this species reveal that flooding rather than predation may now be the major threat to successful nesting. Desiccation can also be a problem, with losses from this cause being reported from Florida. The figure for predation is low in this region, with only 14 per cent of clutches being affected, according to one survey. Fertility is high, with an average of 90 per cent of the eggs containing embryos. This is determined in the field by the presence of bands on the eggs. Previous studies suggest this figure may not be reflected in the hatching rate, however, with less than half the eggs actually developing through to term.

Mortality of the hatchlings is also quite variable, and it has been suggested that the maximum chance of survival to four years of age is less than one in four. Assorted birds, including certain raptors, as well as wading birds, mammals, such as racoons and wild cats, and even some fish will all take young American crocodiles.

The average clutch size is about 40 eggs, although as many as 80 have been recorded at some nests. This suggests that nest-sharing may take place in some areas, with two females laying in the same locality. The eggs themselves measure up to 7.5 cm (3 in) in length and the maximum width is about 5 cm (2 in).

The female generally has a den close to her nest, located in a river bank, with the entrance sometimes below the water level. From here, she will watch over her eggs, attacking other animals which venture too close. Iguanas are sometimes attracted to lay their eggs in the vicinity of crocodile nests, and one American crocodile was observed to seize a dozen such lizards near her nest during the incubation period, which lasts about three months.

As the time for hatching approaches, so a female will rest with her head on the nest, listening for the calls of the hatchlings within. She will then dig them out, using her front feet on this occasion, and may also help some of her offspring out of their eggs, by carefully cracking the shells in her mouth. Others will be picked up directly and carried to the water, with an average of three hatchlings at a time being transported in this manner. If not all of the eggs are ready to hatch, she may then return later to release the other hatchlings.

The actual degree of subsequent parental care in this species is variable, and is influenced by the habitat. Where there is a risk of the young crocodiles dehydrating in hypersaline water, or being washed away by currents, they are usually left on their own soon after they have hatched. They can then disperse, and at least a few may find suitable conditions where they can develop.

Hunting for its skin has previously affected the population of this species, and habitat changes are now adversely affecting some parts of its distribution, such as the Dominican Republic. Here, the diversion of streams feeding into the Lago Enriquillo for irrigation purposes has significantly raised the salinity of this lake. Hatchling American crocodiles are now unable to survive in its waters, which is disastrous for the long-term stability of this important population.

The absence of the American crocodile from certain areas within its range, such as the Bahamas, may also be explained by the inability of hatchlings to survive under conditions of hypersalinity. Although adult crocodiles may swim and breed here, there is no prospect of their offspring surviving, even in the absence of predators, without access to fresh or brackish water.

Since adult crocodiles are much less susceptible to the effects of salt water, it may be that juveniles grow very rapidly to overcome their disadvantage in this respect. In captivity, hatchlings have grown 5 cm (2 in) per month, at least until they have reached 1.4 m (4½ ft) long.

In spite of being protected in Florida, the number of American crocodiles there, on the edge of the species' range, has not risen greatly during recent years. Again, it is possible that, with less fresh water entering Florida Bay because of changes in drainage patterns, the increased salinity may not be tolerated well by young hatchlings, and this might be a growing cause of early mortality.

Loss of habitat is also probably significant, with a noticeable reduction in the species' breeding range since the 1930s. But in at least one area, these crocodiles appear to have adapted to new nesting sites. They are now breeding within the cooling canal system of the Florida Power and Light Company's plant, located at Turkey Point, south of Miami. The crocodiles nest on the spoil berms here and, unmolested by people, a significant breeding group is being established.

The overall population of American crocodiles in the state probably does not exceed 500, and only about 25 females nest here each year. The colony at Turkey Point is now credited with producing about 10 per cent of the youngsters hatched in Florida annually. It is, nevertheless, difficult to gain an accurate picture of the numbers of American crocodiles because they tend to disperse when not breeding, and may travel considerable distances overland. Individuals can move through an area of up to 260 ha (640 acres), and may choose to travel up to 6 km (4 miles) in six days, which makes monitoring of the population both a demanding and expensive task.

MORELET'S CROCODILE *CROCODYLUS MORELETII*

The distribution of this species is centred on the Caribbean side of Central America, where it ranges from the northern part of the State of Tamaulipas in Mexico southwards via the Yucatan Peninsula. It continues through Belize and reaches almost as far as the Motagua River valley in the northern part of Guatemala. It may also extend into the northern area of Honduras, although, almost certainly, reports from the western side of Mexico refer to the American crocodile (*Crocodylus acutus*).

Morelet's crocodile is a relatively small species, which does not exceed 3.5 m ($11\frac{1}{2}$ ft) in length. It inhabits swampland, ponds, lagoons and similar quiet stretches of fresh water, especially where there is dense vegetation. This provides areas where young crocodiles in particular can retreat, while during the dry season, when water levels fall, adults often burrow into the banks and aestivate here until the rains return.

On occasions, these crocodiles have been seen in faster-flowing stretches of water, seeking aquatic snails and other prey, which may include mud turtles (*Kinosternon* species). They also feed on small mammals and fish, with hatchlings tending to take more invertebrate prey.

Named after the zoologist who obtained the first specimen during

Fig. 11   Distribution of Morelet's crocodile (*Crocodylus moreletii*).

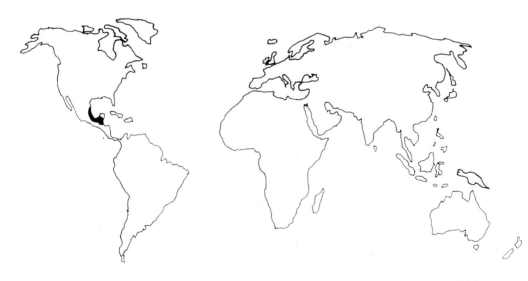

the last century, Morelet's crocodile subsequently became something of an enigma. After the original description of the species had been published in 1851, it was in 1919 that the real confusion arose. During that year, Thomas Barbour observed that snails acquired by Morelet had been incorrectly ascribed as originating from Yucatan (now in Guatemala), whereas in fact they had come from Cuba. He therefore concluded, incorrectly, that the crocodile had also been collected on the island, and so, for a period, *Crocodylus moreletii* became synonymous with the Cuban crocodile (*Crocodylus rhombifer*). Mistakenly, this island was taken to be the locality of the type specimen. Needless to state, no others were obtained here, but it was some years before the error was rectified.

Then in 1924, the situation was finally resolved by Karl P. Schmidt, working for Chicago's Field Museum close to Belize City, in what was then British Honduras (now Belize). Here Schmidt found *Crocodylus moreletii* to be abundant, and was able to reconcile the taxonomic confusion.

There are actually a number of distinctive features which separate these species, not least the fact that Morelet's crocodile has pale silvery brown irides, whereas those of the Cuban crocodile are dark. Its physical appearance is less specialized, with much lighter scaling on the hind legs and, in terms of coloration, Morelet's crocodile is duller, being predominantly greyish brown, offset against some darker markings.

Since the time of Schmidt's visit, the numbers of Morelet's crocodile present throughout its range have declined quite dramatically, and the species is now considered to be endangered. Illegal hunting is the major threat to the continued survival of this species. There are no osteoderms in its belly skin, and so hides can be converted into top-quality leather goods. The scale of past hunting can be gauged from the fact that, over 50 years ago, it was not unusual for up to a 1000 skins to be sold just at Villahermosa market, in the Mexican State of Tabasco during the course of a single day.

In some parts of Mexico today, however, such as the Los Tuxtlas region of Vera Cruz, the species has becomes extinct. A similar severe reduction in numbers can be seen throughout its whole area of distribution. The situation has worsened with increasing development in some regions, because this has enabled professional hunters to penetrate even further into remote parts of the Morelet's crocodile's range. Furthermore, in the past, hunters often left some of the older crocodiles so that they would continue to breed, but now whole populations are decimated with no thought for their future.

Protective measures do exist, but again, enforcement has proved to be difficult. Up until 1981, hides were still being exported from Belize to European destinations, but now this trade has apparently been stopped. A moratorium on hunting, followed by regulated hunting in perhaps a decade's time, has been proposed as the best means of conserving the species in Belize, with protection being given to existing areas of habitat.

It is clear that this species will breed well in captivity, however, and so there is an obvious potential for farming these crocodiles. In Chiapas, Mexico, a group of six adult pairs of Morelet's crocodile has been established at the Tuxtla Guiterrez Zoo, with an annual production of about 60 hatchlings. These are reared for a year and then released, as part of a state reintroduction programme, into areas where the species has previously been wiped out. Other breeding groups are kept at the Atlanta Zoological Park in Georgia and at the Houston Zoo in Texas.

The female Morelet's crocodiles will construct a mound of vegetation, which may be up to 3 m (10 ft) across, and 1 m (3 ft) high, close to water. Occasionally they may even nest on floating debris directly above the water. Egg-laying occurs at the end of the dry season, with a typical clutch comprising of between 20 and 45 eggs, each measuring about 10 cm (4 in) long. There is some evidence to suggest nest-sharing occurs. One nest contained 70 eggs, which were probably laid by two separate females.

It will be about 80 days before the eggs start to hatch, and the female remains nearby throughout this period, finally helping the youngsters from the nest. At this stage, they are about 16 cm (6 in) long, and yellow and black in colour. Males also sometimes assist the female in the early care of hatchlings. It is not unknown for older juveniles to be killed by mature females, fearful that their brood may be cannibalized. Initially, the young crocodiles eat small fish and also hunt crickets and similar invertebrates at the water's edge.

CUBAN CROCODILE *CROCODYLUS RHOMBIFER*

With one of the most restricted distributions of all crocodilians, it is not surprising that this species is seriously endangered. It is present only in the Zapata Swamp, located in Matanzas Province, in Cuba, with another small population occurring on the offshore Isla de la Juventud, in the Lanier Swamp. Cuban crocodiles also used to occur on Grand Cayman Island, up to 800 years ago, but have since vanished from here. In the past, individuals measuring up to 5 m (16 ft) were known, but generally, this species now does not exceed 3.5 m ($11\frac{1}{2}$ ft) in length.

Before hunting of crocodiles became widespread on Cuba, it appears that the Cuban and American crocodiles frequented different habitats. The Cuban species was concentrated in areas of marshland and fresh-

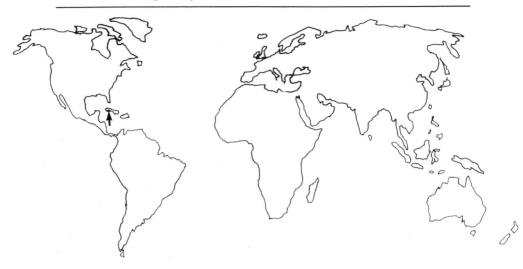

Fig. 12   Distribution of the Cuban crocodile (*Crocodylus rhombifer*).

water swamps, whereas the latter was found more in coastal areas and rivers. Hunting pressures were directed towards the American croco-dile, with its valuable hide, but the growth of charcoal-burning saw the habitat of the Cuban crocodile reduced significantly. It never appears to have been widespread, being concentrated mainly in Matanzas Province, although it also extended further east at this stage as well.

The change in distribution evident today resulted from those early hunting pressures, which enabled the Cuban crocodile to move into areas formerly occupied by its American relative. Unfortunately, this has placed the existence of the Cuban species in peril, rather than securing its future.

The Cuban crocodile has a short and broad head, a noticeable bony ridge behind the eyes and large scales on the legs. The dorsal shield along the back is continuous with the protective covering over the neck, and the body coloration, being a combination of yellow and black spots, is also unusual. But in spite of its distinctive appearance, Cuban crocodiles are hybridizing with the remnants of the American crocodile population, as both now occur in the same environment.

Known locally as *mixturados*, these offspring display characteristics of both parents, with an intermediate skull structure in some cases, although extremes are known, where an individual resembles an American crocodile in terms of head shape, but its Cuban ancestor in coloration.

The problem of hybridization was worsened a quarter of a century ago, when as many surviving Cuban crocodiles as possible were moved under governmental orders to special *corrales*, located at the Laguna del Tesoro. Here in the Zapata Swamp, they interbred with American crocodiles, and there may now be more hybrids than pure Cuban crocodiles in existence.

Unfortunately, the other locality where the species occurs, in the Lanier Swamp in the vicinity of Siguanea Bay, has since been colonized by introduced dusky caimans (*Caiman crocodilus fuscus*). These represent a distinct threat to hatchling Cuban crocodiles, preying upon them. These caimans could therefore clearly endanger the existing population of crocodiles over a number of years.

In terms of lifestyle, it appears that Cuban crocodiles now feed mainly on fish, and on the turtles which occur widely through the island. The flattened, relatively broad teeth in the back of the crocodile's mouth are thought to be employed in crushing the shell of these chelonians. But the enlarged, powerful teeth nearer the front of the jaws puzzled zoologists, since they appeared to have no obvious function, although presumably they evolved for a specific purpose.

Fossil evidence provided the necessary clues to unravel this mystery, dating back to a stage when these crocodiles were more widespread on Cuba than they have been during recent historic times. The remains of huge ground sloths have been unearthed. These were essentially vegetarian (but protected by powerful claws and sharp teeth), with some reaching the size of a bear. It is clear from the fossilized remains that there was definite interaction between the giant ground sloths and Cuban crocodiles. Their bones have been found together and, significantly, the remains of such sloths show injuries which were sustained from bites of these crocodiles.

Clearly, to prey upon such a formidable adversary, the crocodile needed to evolve additional protection, as well as the means to dispatch its prey with minimum risk. The blunt rear teeth could then have been used to crush the sloths' bones, as they are used for turtles' shells today. Significantly, the Cuban crocodile is well equipped for hunting on land. Its legs are well muscled, with the feet themselves being short, and there is little webbing between the toes.

They move in the characteristic 'high walk' fashion more than other species. This was probably sufficient to enable them to catch sloths, which themselves were far from agile creatures. The appearance of the Cuban crocodile today is thus a direct reflection of its past lifestyle, and it can truly be described as a living fossil.

The hope must be that captive breeding will ensure its survival. In this case, however, it is doubtful, particularly in view of its limited distribution and propensity for hybridization, that reintroduction to the wild on any scale will prove feasible. There is a reasonable zoo population of the species, however, and breeding projects are under way, so that at least numbers of the Cuban crocodile can be maintained for the foreseeable future.

ORINOCO CROCODILE *CROCODYLUS INTERMEDIUS*

The characteristic feature of this species is the narrow snout which slopes upwards towards its tip. As a further means of identification, the dorsal armour of the Orinoco crocodile is symmetrical, with six prominent scutes present on the back of the neck. It is otherwise somewhat similar to the American species, although it can grow significantly larger, according to reports from the last century. Individuals measuring almost 7 m ($22\frac{1}{2}$ ft) were then not unknown, although the biggest males today rarely exceed 5 m (16 ft) in length.

Orinoco crocodiles evolved in conjunction with the river system of the same name and inhabit both Venezuela and the eastern part of Colombia. During the wet season, they often move overland to quieter stretches of water, such as lakes, returning to deep stretches of the river as these localities dry up.

Fish, as well as small mammals, such as capybaras and birds, form the bulk of the diet, with younger individuals taking a higher proportion of invertebrate prey, including crabs, snails and beetles. Although reputed to take people occasionally, actual attacks appear to be very rare. This may be a reflection of the severe decline in the crocodile population during recent years, however, which has resulted in an abundance of prey.

Fig. 13   Distribution of the Orinoco crocodile (*Crocodylus intermedius*).

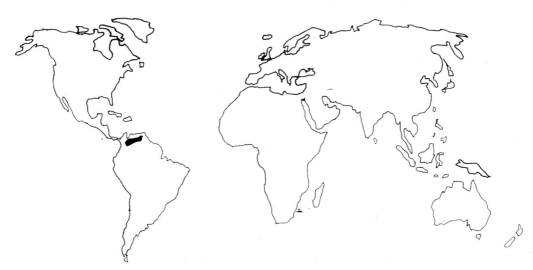

While no precise figures are available, it is clear that there may well have been hundreds of thousands of these crocodiles in Colombia before European settlement began in earnest. Recent studies suggest that the species is now literally on the verge of extinction in this country, with the total population comprising no more than 500 individuals. A similar situation exists in Venezuela, where the number of Orinoco crocodiles probably does not exceed 1000 in total.

This devastating decline can be traced back to the 1920s, when hunting became widespread. The large size of these crocodiles, and the high quality of their belly skin, which is free from osteoderms, meant that hunters could make a fortune from killing these crocodiles. The numbers taken are staggering, with one dealer alone purchasing 4000 hides daily at the height of the slaughter, which extended from the late 1920s to the early 1930s. By 1948, the crocodiles had become so scarce that it was no longer economic to hunt them on a commercial basis.

Nesting takes place early in the year, with the female digging a simple hole. Here she will lay possibly as many as 70 eggs, although this may be the results of two clutches laid by separate females. The site chosen is close to water, but above the high-water area, on a suitable sandbank. Predation by teiid lizards and black vultures (*Coragyps atratus*) can reduce the number of nests, although females generally remain close to the nest, as a deterrent. Hatching takes place about two months later, and the young crocodiles are protected by their mother for a further period afterwards.

On rare occasions, Orinoco crocodiles have been found on islands such as Trinidad and Grenada, which are located about 241 km (150 miles) to the north of Venezuela. Almost certainly, these crocodiles have been swept out to sea on floodwater, possibly travelling for part of their journey on rafts of vegetation. The reason why the species has never penetrated into the Amazon basin from the Orinoco remains a mystery, however, but it seems rather late for any such colonization to occur, in view of its imperilled status.

Orinoco crocodiles have been bred at various localities in Venezuela, and a small captive breeding programme is also under way in Colombia. These offer some hope for the species' future, with a breeding group also present at the Metro Zoo in Miami, Florida. The problem of illegal hunting still menaces the existing wild populations, however, with the skin itself being rather similar to that of the American crocodile, which can pose enforcement difficulties.

NILE CROCODILE *CROCODYLUS NILOTICUS*

Although this species' range has contracted during recent historical

157

Plate 69   The Orinoco crocodile (*Crocodylus intermedius*) is tan in colour and much lighter than its American counterpart.

times, it still occurs widely through much of Africa, to the south of the Sahara Desert. Hunting has taken its toll. Nile crocodiles used to be quite common on the major islands in the Seychelles, such as Mahé and Silhouette, but were eliminated from these restricted habitats early in the 1800s. They were also present on the Comoros. In some areas, notably southern and northern parts of Africa, the reduction in range has resulted from the spread of increasingly arid conditions rather than hunting pressures.

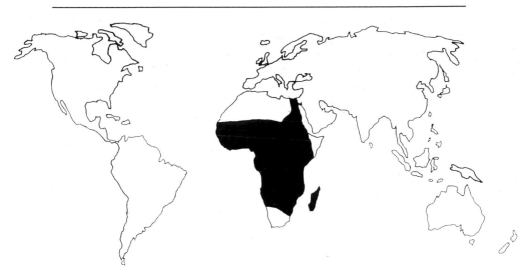

Fig. 14   Distribution of the Nile crocodile (*Crocodylus niloticus*).

The species has also withdrawn progressively from the River Nile itself, having first vanished from the delta here during the 1700s. It remained in the vicinity of Cairo, although by 1870, the Nile crocodile no longer occurred below Aswan, which marks the first falls on the river. Barely a century later, in 1972, it was deemed extinct in Egypt, but since the building of the Aswan Dam, Nile crocodiles have begun to recolonize this region.

Other significant populations have built up again in Kenya, following the prohibition of hunting, which was introduced in 1955. The only area where crocodiles escaped this pressure was around Lake Turkana. In this remote locality, Nile crocodiles evolved pronounced osteoderms on their ventral surface, which meant that they were of little value for the skin trade.

On occasion, these crocodiles can be encountered on Kenyan beaches, and may even be swept out to sea. Some have reached the island of Zanzibar and, almost certainly, this was how the species reached other islands off the eastern coast of Africa, including the Malagasy Republic (Madagascar), from other coastal areas further south.

The past presence of the Nile crocodile in Israel and the southwestern areas of Syria is less certain. Further afield, in Turkey, close to Caesarea (Kayseri), there is a river which is still called Crocodile River by the local people, but their occurrence here is unclear. It is known that remnant populations in north Africa have died out quite recently. In southern Algeria, for example, as the lakes of Wadi Iherir receded,

159

the Nile crocodile remained in this central Saharan part of its former range into the 1930s. Slightly further south, in the Ennedi Mountain district of north-eastern Chad, the species still survived in the early 1960s, although it is most unlikely that any remain here today. Throughout the country, Nile crocodiles have been ruthlessly hunted.

In view of the wide range over which the species still occurs, it is not surprising that there appear to be regional differences between populations, although taxonomists still tend to group all these forms together. Today, large Nile crocodiles are not frequently reported, and males rarely exceed 5 m (16 ft) in length.

But much bigger individuals have been known, with the largest on record being shot in 1905 by the Duke of Mecklenberg. Obtained near Mwanza in Tanzania, this particular crocodile was $6\frac{1}{2}$ m ($21\frac{1}{4}$ ft) long and probably weighed not less than 1043 kg (2300 lb). The official record stands at 5.94 m ($19\frac{1}{2}$ ft) however, and was established in 1953. Shot by a member of Uganda's Game and Fisheries Department on the Semliki River, this giant crocodilian's girth was 2.24 m ($7\frac{1}{4}$ ft).

Nile crocodiles are certainly dangerous predators, and probably kill at least 300 people every year in Africa, although worldwide, they are marginally less of a threat than the Indo-Pacific species. Adults in particular are opportunistic feeders, taking virtually any bird or animal which comes within striking distance when they are hungry. As an example, a notorious crocodile, christened *Kwena* by the locals, was killed by a hunter called Bobby Wilmot, in Botswana's Okavango Swamp during November 1968. Measuring some 5.87 m ($19\frac{1}{4}$ ft), its body was found to contain the remains of a local woman, minus the limbs, two goats and about half a donkey.

The hunting technique of the Nile crocodile ensures that even large game, such as giraffes, can be taken effectively. The reptile lurks unseen near a spot in the river where the animals come to drink, suddenly rushing forward and seizing its prey by the head. But these crocodiles can sometimes bite off more than they can safely swallow, with one juvenile individual choking to death on a large turtle which jammed in its throat. At this juvenile stage, fish often form the bulk of the crocodile's diet rather than large mammals.

There appears to be a fairly rigorous social structure within groups of Nile crocodiles. Hatchlings remain shy and tend to conceal themselves in quiet stretches of water, feeding largely on insects, as well as amphibians. Once they have grown to about 1 m ($3\frac{1}{4}$ ft), by which stage they will be about two years old, the youngsters move into deeper water, and associate in groups of up to 20 individuals, remaining away from adults in the vicinity.

Gradually, they start to integrate into adult communities, which are typically dominated by a large bull. He selects his favoured basking site, with others of the group then following on to the river bank. Should they be challenged by a larger male, the youngsters will indicate their submission by raising their head upright out of the water and then submerging.

The dominant male may mate with most of the females in the group, although in some parts of the range monogamy appears to be more common. Nile crocodiles will generally breed for the first time at between 12 and 15 years of age. Females excavate their nest using their hind legs for this purpose, and may then choose to use the same site during successive years. Clutch size can vary from just 16 eggs up to 80 or more in the case of larger individuals.

Both male and female often guard the nest site once the incubation period has commenced, with the female rarely feeding through this phase, which lasts for about three months. The young are then dug out of the nest by the female, and remain together as a group, guarded by their parents for up to two months. The call of a hatchling will elicit a protective response not only from its parents, but also from other crocodiles in the area, reflecting a high degree of social organization. Their mother also signals danger by vibrating her flanks quickly, with the waves passing through the water to her offspring, alerting them to the threat.

After this phase, the hatchlings will then avoid larger crocodiles and start to live on their own. The rainy period will have created temporary pools of water and these will be teeming with insects and other small prey. But when winter comes, the young will burrow into suitable banks, often in small groups and cease feeding. Nile crocodiles may also bury themselves in the base of muddy pools as they dry up, awaiting the return of the rains.

With their fearsome reputation, it is perhaps not surprising that so much interest has been focused on the presence of birds feeding and pecking with apparent immunity inside the mouths of Nile crocodiles. Such behaviour was first described over 1100 years ago. The birds, which benefit from picking at the remains of food on the teeth of crocodiles, as well as removing numerous parasites, are primarily the spur-winged plover (*Vanellus spingsus*) and the thick-knee (*Burhinus senegalensis*). A further bonus for the crocodile may be that the sudden unexpected departure of the birds gives an indication of possible danger. Predator and potential prey peacefully co-exist under these circumstances, with the birds probably being fast enough in most cases to escape, even if the crocodile did become hostile.

The Nile crocodile has, during the present century, withstood a remarkable level of human predation, with an estimated three million individuals being killed for their skins between 1950 and 1980 alone. Other dangers now include habitat modification and accidental kills. In Natal for example, Lake St Lucia is becoming increasingly saline, because of water being removed for irrigation purposes upstream, and this is known to have already resulted in crocodile deaths. Meanwhile, on Lake Turkana in Kenya, fishing with gill nets is now entrapping crocodiles under water and drowning them. Careful monitoring of Nile populations needs to be continued and hunting quotas strictly enforced to maintain the species' present distribution for the future.

AFRICAN SLENDER-SNOUTED CROCODILE
CROCODYLUS CATAPHRACTUS

Present in western and central parts of Africa, this species is unusual in a number of respects. The protective scales over the neck are present in four rows rather than the two rows found in other *Crocodylus* species, and also, uniquely, merge with the dorsal armour. The markings on the jaws are more akin to those seen in various caimans and the false gharial (*Tomistoma schlegelii*) than related members of the genus *Crocodylus*.

The habits of the African slender-snouted crocodile are not well known, partly because the species occurs in remote forested areas, which makes study difficult. It also has been reported from coastal

Fig. 15   Distribution of the African slender-snouted crocodile (*Crocodylus cataphractus*).

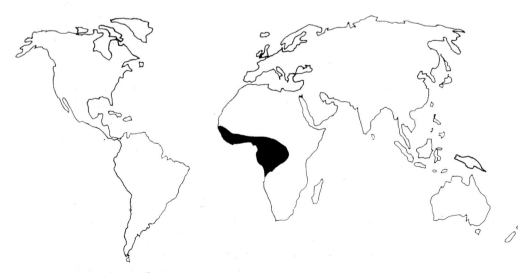

regions on occasions, and was once encountered on Bioko Island, which is located 45 km (28 miles) into the Atlantic, off the Cameroon coast of West Africa. These crocodiles may grow up to 4 m (13 ft) long, although they average about 2.5 m (8 ft) in length. They appear to live relatively solitary lives, never being found at high densities, even in areas where the habitat appears favourable.

Recent studies conducted in the Ivory Coast have revealed the African slender-snouted crocodile to be most commonly encountered in stretches of open water, including lakes, lagoons and rivers. It appears to be highly aquatic and presumably feeds on a variety of fish, amphibians and crustaceans. Nesting begins at the end of the dry season, when there is a good covering of leaves on the forest floor to build the mound. The nest is usually sited close to a small stream, with egg-laying following within a week of the structure being completed.

Clutch size is small, averaging just 16 eggs, although up to 23 have been known. Each measures about 81.5 cm ($3\frac{1}{4}$ in) in length. Hatching takes place within 16 weeks and, although the female usually remains in the vicinity, she is very shy, and will not tolerate a close approach. She is instrumental in helping her offspring from the nest, however, and will subsequently respond to their calls.

They may face a number of predators, including soft-shelled turtles (*Trionyx triungius*) but, generally, losses appear to be low. This may account for the relatively small number of eggs laid, compared with other crocodilians. The young will feed at first on aquatic invertebrates, but as they grow, they will start to take larger prey, with their narrow snout making them effective predators in an aquatic environment. Their size will ultimately enable them to deal with bigger mammals, including *Colobus* monkeys, should they come within reach.

The status of the African slender-snouted crocodile is unclear. It is officially protected through much of its range. Yet these crocodiles are killed for food, and their skins may be used locally, although these do not appear to have been in demand for international trade. Nevertheless, as the numbers of Nile crocodiles throughout their area of distribution have been reduced for this reason, so populations of the African slender-snouted crocodile may be considered more vulnerable to poachers.

INDO-PACIFIC CROCODILE *CROCODYLUS POROSUS*

Found over a wide area, from south-east Asia south via Indonesia to northern parts of Australia, ranging also to the Philippines and eastwards as far as the Solomon Islands and Vanuatu, this highly adaptable species is also the largest surviving species of crocodilian.

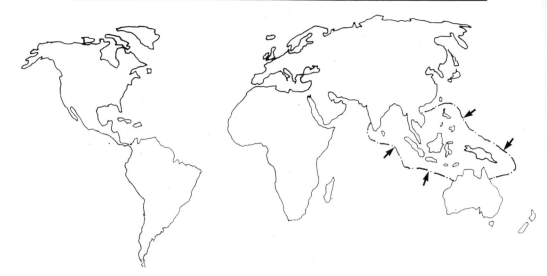

Fig. 16   Distribution of the Indo-Pacific crocodile (*Crocodylus porosus*).

Indeed, there are stories of Indo-Pacific crocodiles exceeding 9 m (30 ft), but these have never been reliably documented. One of the most convincing dates back to the 1920s and originates from the Segama River in northern Borneo, where a number of giant Indo-Pacific crocodiles have been reported.

A rubber plantation owner called James Montgomery described a huge individual which the local Seluke tribe believed to be over 200 years old. On one occasion, Montgomery saw the reptile on a sandbank in the river. It was resting with its head in the water at one end, and its tail slightly submerged at the other. When it moved off, he measured the length of the sandbank, which was 10 m (32 ft 10 in). This in turn suggested that the crocodile measured 10.05 m (33 ft) long. The Seluke considered this crocodile to be the father of the devil, and always threw silver into the river to protect themselves from evil when he was seen.

In Australia, the largest Indo-Pacific crocodile recorded here was harpooned in the MacArthur River, close to Barroloola in the Northern Territory. It measured 6.15 m (20 ft 2 in) when killed on 26 June 1960. Another individual, just 5 cm (2 in) shorter, was killed also in Northern Territory two years later, when it began to attack farmstock. It weighed an amazing 1097 kg (2418 lb). Few such large crocodiles probably remain, although some have been obtained in Papua New Guinea during recent years. One giant was drowned in fishermen's nets at Obo on the Fly River, during 1979. It measured 6.2 m (20 ft 4 in). Within the Bhitarkanika Sanctuary, in Orissa, India, there is a huge male today which exceeds 7 m (23 ft). It is certainly feasible, therefore,

164

on this evidence that these crocodiles could grow as large as 9 m (30 ft), making them truly fearsome predators.

Although better known in the past as both the saltwater and estuarine crocodile, this species actually occurs in freshwater habitats as well, and so the description of 'Indo-Pacific' is more accurate. Nevertheless, it is not unusual to see odd individuals in the sea, and they may cover considerable distances. A male measuring 3.8 m ($12\frac{1}{4}$ ft) was encountered on Ponape, part of the eastern Caroline group of islands, at least 1360 km (845 miles) away from an existing population. At sea, Indo-Pacific crocodiles appear to prefer drifting rather than active swimming and presumably, in the past, this has helped them to colonize many islands.

They can also be found in freshwater localities, up to 1130 km (700 miles) from the sea and, wherever they are encountered, they are dangerous to people. Over 40 holiday-makers were killed by these crocodiles during December 1975 when their boat sank on the Malili River in Sulawesi (Celebes), Indonesia, and, from the available evidence, it is clear this species may kill 1000 people a year through its wide range.

Large Indo-Pacific crocodiles will take virtually any animal, including feral buffaloes in Australia, wild boar (*Sus scrofa*) and rhesus monkeys (*Macaca mulatta*) in India, and a variety of fish, including sharks, as well as turtles, birds and domestic livestock. The breeding season varies according to the area concerned, being earlier in the year in the northern part of its range.

Males will be mature when they reach a size of about 3.2 m ($10\frac{1}{4}$ ft), generally at about 16 years of age. Females mature at a smaller size, when they are about 2.2 m (7 ft) in length, by which stage they will be about ten years old. Nesting generally takes place during the wet season, with the female constructing a mound of vegetation, often mixing this with a liberal amount of mud. Billabongs are favoured sites in Australia but, where the species has been heavily persecuted, the crocodiles retreat to remote areas where they can nest unmolested.

By the time that the nest is complete, it will measure about 2.5 m (8 ft) across and as much as 91 cm (3 ft) in height. Here between 25 and 90 eggs will be laid. As in other species, the fertile egg develops a distinctive opaque band, caused by the fusion of the extra-embryonic membranes to the shell, around its centre. Incubation lasts for about 90 days, during which time, the female remains nearby in a wallow and will not hesitate to attack if the nest is threatened. Monitor lizards (*Varanus* species) will sometimes prey on crocodile nests, as will some other animals, including wild pigs.

When the young crocodiles are due to hatch, the female will dig down to the egg chamber, about 20 cm (4 in) below the surface of the mound, and free them. She then carries them to the water. The individual size of eggs between clutches is quite variable, and this has a distinct bearing on the size of the hatchlings. In the Indo-Pacific species, as with other crocodiles, double-yolked eggs are known, with their incidence being estimated at 0.1 per cent in this case. Although two embryos may develop, they are not likely to prove viable, even if they do ultimately hatch. Losses amongst healthy hatchlings are surprisingly large in this species, while excessive flooding can cause wipe-out of nests in some areas, before the end of the incubation period.

As the numbers of sub-adult and adult crocodiles have risen in Australia, so it is evident that juvenile mortality in general has increased. Young hatchlings face predators, such as snake-necked turtles (Chelidae), and even Johnston's crocodiles in areas where the two species share the same habitat. But young crocodiles are at further risk from bigger individuals, quite apart from hunting pressures in some areas. Research in Australia has suggested that, overall, half the hatchlings will die in their first year, with less than 1 per cent surviving to maturity.

Hunting has had a major effect on the overall population of this species, and losses of larger individuals have seriously compromised its reproductive success, worsening its decline in some areas. The small scute size and absence of osteoderms has meant that the hides of these crocodiles are highly valued in the leather trade. It is hard to curb hunting, even if there are legal measures, when a hide can fetch the equivalent of six months' wages in a country like Thailand.

Ranching and farming, by lessening the demand for skins from wild-caught crocodilians, can offer hope to existing populations. Removal of eggs is clearly possible without having any detrimental long-term effects on the status of the species but, in some areas, Indo-Pacific crocodiles also face major habitat changes.

In Australia, for example, feral buffaloes are becoming a major menace, by destroying the crocodiles' nesting habitat in Northern Territory. Relatively large numbers of crocodiles are also being killed in fishermen's nets here and elsewhere. The natural antipathy to these crocodiles throughout their range also remains a significant factor which makes conservation measures difficult to enforce effectively, without the support of the local people.

MUGGER   *CROCODYLUS PALUSTRIS*

The distribution of this crocodile is centred on the Indian subcontinent, where it is present in India, as well as in Nepal, Pakistan, Iran and possibly Bangladesh. A separate population is also present in

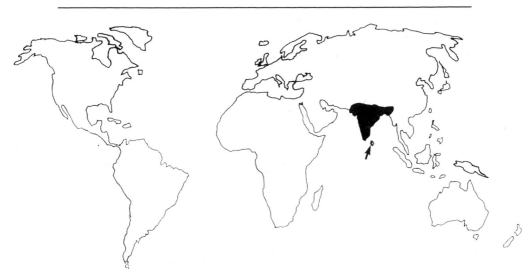

Fig. 17   Distribution of the mugger (*Crocodylus palustrus*).

Sri Lanka. This large species can grow to about 4 m (13 ft) long, although generally today, adults measure between 1.8–2.4 m (6–8 ft). The mugger is rather reminiscent of an alligator in terms of its appearance, as well as its lifestyle.

Its alternative name of marsh crocodile stems from its scientific name, with *palustris* translating as 'of the marshes'. It tends to be found in areas of relatively shallow water, which may explain the apparent development of enlarged scutes around the throat. As in the alligators, these provide protection when the crocodile moves through its habitat. Muggers are usually encountered in areas of fresh water, but are also sometimes seen in brackish water. On occasions, when the pools dry up, these crocodiles will move overland in search of more permanent areas of water.

The mugger (a name derived from Hindustani) is also characterized by its broad snout, reinforcing its similarity to alligators. It feeds on amphibians, as well as birds and mammals, including various monkeys and squirrels. These crocodiles have learnt to steal fish, especially catfish, from nets.

Being an adaptable species, the mugger has colonized man-made lakes, called tanks, notably in Sri Lanka where no natural freshwater lakes are present. They are rarely found in water deeper than 5 m (16 ft) and avoid fast-flowing rivers, especially during the rainy season.

Females may start breeding once they reach 1.7 m ($5\frac{1}{2}$ ft) long, during their sixth year, while males are larger, about 2.6 m ($8\frac{1}{2}$ ft) and older, around ten years of age, before they will mate for the first time. A male may mate with several females in succession. A sloping bank is a popular nesting site, with the female digging a simple hole, where the eggs will be buried. A typical clutch comprises about 30 eggs, although as many as 46 is not unknown. These are generally laid between the end of February and early April. It can take 65 days for the eggs to hatch, and the hatchlings, measuring up to 30 cm (12 in), are ultimately freed by the female.

The number of muggers has fallen considerably in some parts of its range during recent years, but now conservation schemes being operated in many parts of India are proving worthwhile. Eggs are harvested from the wild and hatched in captivity, with the resulting offspring then being released back in suitable areas of habitat. This repopulation effort first bore fruit at the Nagarjuna Sagar-Srisailam Sanctuary, located at the Ethipothala Falls on the Chandravanka River. Here, following the release of eight muggers up to six years old between 1977 and 1980, a female laid nine eggs with four hatching on 13 June 1981. This success was achieved in an area where muggers had vanished over 15 years beforehand.

A number of zoos are also breeding this species and, with increasing habitat protection, the mugger's future is more secure. Traditional demand for the mugger as a source of medicinal remedies, however, still remains a problem, while fishing by means of gill nets also endangers local populations. Habitat destruction and modification elsewhere in its range, in Sri Lanka for example, where the mugger is also killed for food, may affect long-term reproductive success, especially when

Fig.18   Distribution of the New Guinea crocodile (*Crocodylus novaeguineae*).

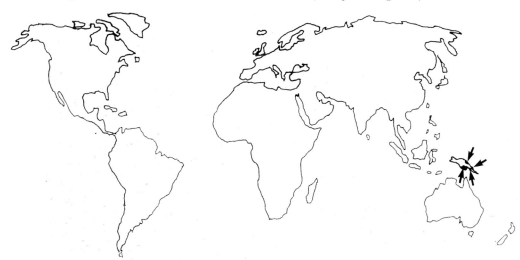

hatchlings are then forced to cross large tracts of land in search of water.

NEW GUINEA CROCODILE *CROCODYLUS NOVAEGUINEAE*

It was not until 1908 that a skull of this species was obtained and brought from Papua New Guinea, although for many years, it remained effectively unidentified, since it was believed that only the Indo-Pacific crocodile occurred here. The division between the two species was first hinted at in a paper written by C.W.A. Monckton, who had lived in New Guinea for many years. He was of the opinion that there was a smaller, relatively inoffensive species, as well as the Indo-Pacific crocodile, living on the island. Examination of the original skull obtained two decades earlier finally confirmed Monckton's view in 1928, although the discovery was not universally accepted at this time.

It is now clear that the New Guinea crocodile is a distinct species, found in areas of fresh water and growing up to 4 m (13 ft) long. Its snout is relatively narrow, but not as pronounced as that of Johnston's crocodile, which it otherwise tends to resemble in coloration, being brownish with darker bands on the body and tail.

Although on rare occasions it may be found in coastal areas, the New Guinea crocodile does not occur alongside the Indo-Pacific species. The original discovery was made in the vicinity of the lower Sepik River, on the northern coast. It is clear that the southern population, separated by the chain of mountains which divides New Guinea in a

Plate 70   The New Guinea crocodile (*Crocodylus novaeguineae*) was once hunted to the verge of extinction, but now it is increasing in numbers again.

169

horizontal direction along the length of the island, is somewhat different from this northern race, and these two populations do not interbreed. This may well lead to a subspecific division in the future. The species is also said to be present on the Aru Islands, located about 130 km (80 miles) to the west of New Guinea, although this now appears to be doubtful.

Observations about the habits of this species have been difficult to obtain, partly because of the remote areas in which it now occurs, but more significantly, because it is essentially nocturnal in its habits. It is rarely seen basking on land during the day, remaining hidden in the water. Here it hunts fish, amphibians, reptiles and waterbirds, such as coots and rails.

The numbers of the New Guinea crocodile were seriously threatened at one point by the skin trade, and they are scarce in some areas today as a result. Lowland grass swamps are believed to be the main refuge for this species, with individuals only moving into river systems when the water level falls during the dry season.

Breeding activity begins just before the first rains in the north, with females proving to be mound-nesters. Males become more territorial at this time, and following mating, egg-laying occurs about two weeks later, once the nest is completed. The site chosen may be well hidden under trees, or nests may actually be built on a dense mat of grass, floating at the water's surface. Up to 45 eggs may be laid here, with 30 being about the average, depending on the area concerned. The female stays near the nest, but may not actually defend it.

As the young hatch, about 12 weeks later, both males and females will assist them and take them to water. Females then tend to become more territorial, keeping their hatchlings together. Newly hatched crocodiles actively seek warm areas for basking, and this may stimulate early feeding activity. Invertebrates are important in their diet at this stage, with grasshoppers being a favourite item.

Young females mature from about six years of age onwards, by which time they will be nearly 2 m ($6\frac{1}{2}$ ft) long. Males may be slightly bigger, and presumably have to establish themselves in the hierarchy before mating, by which time they could be ten years old. It is difficult to assess the status of this species, but recent indications suggest a recovery in numbers, at least in certain parts of its range. Effective regulation of trade in the skins of this species will be critical to its long-term survival and ranching needs to be linked to on-going field studies in the wild.

JOHNSTON'S CROCODILE *CROCODYLUS JOHNSTONI*

Confined to the northern-tropical area of Australia, this species is also known as the Australian freshwater crocodile. It ranges from north-eastern Queensland via northern parts of Northern Territory, as far as the Fitzroy River in the Kimberley region of Western Australia. Growing to about 3 m (10 ft) in length, this crocodile has a distinctive narrow snout, quite unlike that of the Indo-Pacific crocodile which can be found in the same area. It is generally light brown in colour, with bands of dark spots across the body, which become solid across the tail.

Although heavily hunted in the past, Johnston's crocodile appears to have colonized tidal areas where the Indo-Pacifiic crocodile has been eliminated. Such waters may have a saline content of up to 25 parts per 1000, so clearly this is not exclusively a freshwater species. Relatively aquatic by nature, Johnston's crocodile hunts amphibians, fish and

Plate 71   Johnston's crocodile (*Crocodylus johnstoni*) used to be hunted for its hide, but this practice is now outlawed, although the species is ranched successfully for its hides in Australia.

turtles, and may seize birds and mammals on occasions, although it is not considered to be a threat to people. Its hunting technique appears to be quite passive, with the crocodile often waiting for fish and other prey to come within range. Then, with its light, manoeuvrable snout, it will reach out and seize the creature. Feeding, and hence growth, occurs predominantly during the wet season, with vegetation often being present in their stomachs at this stage.

Dwarf populations have been identified in some areas, as with Nile crocodiles. In this instance, such crocodiles have been obtained in the Liverpool River in Arnhem Land, with the largest individual being a male which measured just 1.53 m (5 ft) long, and weighed 9 kg (20 lb). The biggest mature female was 1.3 m (4 ft), weighing in at 6 kg (13 lb).

Studies suggest that in this area, faced with a long-term shortage of food, the population has evolved to breed at a smaller size. These particular crocodiles also tend to be darker in coloration. Tracking the Johnston's crocodile along the length of this river, it is evident that the average size falls progressively as one moves upstream, and this can be linked directly with a reduction in prey species as well.

Johnston's crocodile is a hole-nester, laying during the dry season. Males are generally not mature until they are 1.65 m (5¼ ft) long, and females measure at least 1.45 m (5 ft) before breeding for the first time. At least in some parts of their range, they may nest in groups. Eighteen nests have been discovered at one such site on the MacKinlay River in Northern Territory, with the eggs being buried 12 cm (5 in) or more, and frequently over 20 cm (8 in), below the surface.

Fig.19   Distribution of Johnston's crocodile (*Crocodylus johnstoni*).

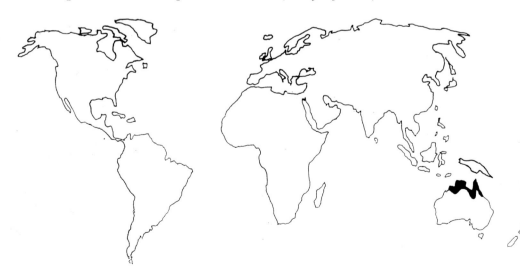

The hatchlings emerge after about 12 weeks, but in this case, the female shows little interest in the nest site, only returning when the young need to be dug out. She will then supervise them in the water. Clutch size is small, ranging from just 4 to 18 eggs, and many nests succumb to predators, such as monitor lizards (*Varanus* species). Only 30 per cent of eggs laid will yield hatchlings, and again, barely 1 per cent of these will survive to maturity. Cannibalism appears to be relatively common in this species, possibly because of a natural shortage of food in some areas. After surviving through to ten years of age, however, individuals may then live without fear of predation (except by human beings) for up to half a century. Following heavy hunting pressure, the numbers of these crocodiles are now showing encouraging signs of recovery.

PHILIPPINE CROCODILE   *CROCODYLUS MINDORENSIS*

Occurring on the Philippine islands of Luzon, Mindoro, Masbate, Busuanga, Samar, Negros, Jolo and Mindanao, this is one of the most critically endangered crocodiles in the world. Its total population may be as low as 500 individuals, with the maximum not exceeding 1000. It is already possibly extinct on the islands of Jolo, Busuanga and Masbate. The last remaining stronghold of the Philippine crocodile appears to be in the Sulu Archipelago, and on Mindanao, although nowhere are large numbers still present. A widespread overall reduction in population makes the likelihood of breeding success and recovery less likely.

Fig. 20   Distribution of the Philippine crocodile (*Crocodylus mindorensis*).

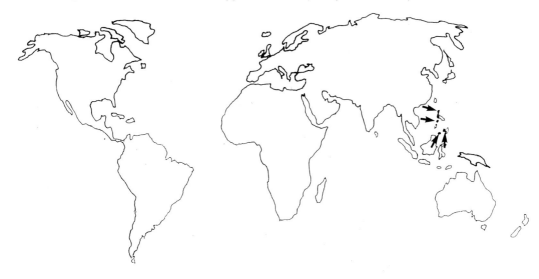

Hunting provided the initial reason for the decline of the species, but now, possibly because of its rarity, this is no longer the major threat. Instead, island development schemes for agricultural purposes have endangered the remaining individuals. The only glimmer of hope is that the previously undocumented existence of Philippine crocodiles on the Visayan Islands in the central Philippines has recently been confirmed, although population data from here are sparse as yet.

The Philippine crocodile is a relatively small species, believed not to exceed 3 m (10 ft) in length. It is found in fresh water and probably preys on fish and other aquatic creatures, as well as small birds and mammals. Little has been documented about its breeding habits, but females build a nest mound, at the end of the dry season. This typically measures 1.5 m (5 ft) in diameter and stands 0.4 m ($1\frac{1}{4}$ ft) high. The clutch size appears to be small, varying from just 7 to 14 eggs in total. The female will guard the nest through the incubation period of about 12 weeks.

It has been suggested that the Philippine crocodile and the New Guinea crocodile should be classified as subspecies, with the New Guinea form being the nominate rate. Recent taxonomic thinking has tended to discard this viewpoint, with the Philippine crocodile having been accorded full specific status for the first time in 1935.

Captive-breeding projects are now under way in an attempt to save the Philippine crocodile from extinction. This is being co-ordinated at Silliman University, and backed by field studies, with the view to establishing a safe refuge for them in the future. A major problem is that, although not implicated as a threat to people, the occurrence of the Philippine crocodile alongside the Indo-Pacific species means that the native people have a strong dislike of these reptiles. This will be difficult to overcome, but is likely to prove a crucial factor in the battle to save the Philippine crocodile from extinction.

SIAMESE CROCODILE   *CROCODYLUS SIAMENSIS*

This is another highly endangered species, which is virtually extinct in the wild. It used to range over a fairly extensive area of south-east Asia, from Vietnam, Cambodia, Thailand and probably southern Laos down to the Malay Peninsula, although absent from west Malaysia. It is also known to have occurred on certain Indonesian islands, although as far as can be ascertained, this crocodile is no longer found on Java, but may possibly survive elsewhere, on Sumatra or Kalimantan. The only definite wild population, numbering less than 50 individuals is present at the Bung Boraphet Reservoir, in the Province of Nakhon Sawan, Thailand.

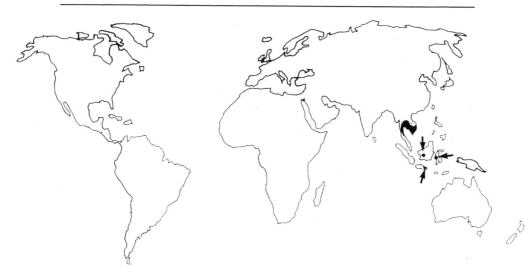

Fig. 21   Distribution of the Siamese crocodile (*Crocodylus siamensis*).

Siamese crocodiles are somewhat similar to the Indo-Pacific species in appearance, but can be distinguished on the basis of their broader snouts. Their throat scales are also more transverse and in terms of size, they do not exceed 4 m (13 ft). This crocodile is predominantly a fresh-water species, found in areas of marshland and lakes, as well as rivers, and it may possibly have ranged into brackish water.

Fish forms the major part of its diet, although it may also take various amphibians and reptiles, and possibly small mammals, in view of its relatively broad snout. The Siamese crocodile was not a species which was aggressive towards people, but it was being ruthlessly hunted even quite early during the present century. In Thailand at this stage, it appears to have been relatively common, both in central parts of the country and certainly in the Patani River. By the 1940s, however, its numbers in Thailand, which appears to have been the centre of its distribution, had fallen significantly. There have never been wide-spread reports of this species from Indonesia. More recently, habitat modification in Thailand has become a major threat to the surviving wild population, with rice growing having reduced their last major stronghold from an area of 25,000 ha (12,355 acres) down to just 5000 ha (2470 acres).

Captive breeding has now greatly benefited this species, however, with the Samutprakan Crocodile Farm holding around 16,000 individuals. There is a need to ensure that a pure strain of the Siamese croco-dile is maintained, since, for commercial reasons, hybrids produced by crossing Siamese and Indo-Pacific crocodiles are desirable, because they have better growth rates and generally provide a superior return.

It appears that April and May are the laying months for the Siamese crocodile, with the female preparing a mound for her eggs. Clutch size may vary from 25 to 50 eggs, and hatching occurs after about 11 weeks. The female watches over the nest and assists the hatchlings as they emerge from the eggs. It seems that Siamese crocodiles are relatively slow to mature, rarely breeding for the first time in captivity before they are ten years old. If suitable, safe habitats could be found, it may well be possible to reintroduce this species back to the wild in the future.

DWARF CROCODILE *OSTEOLAEMUS TETRASPIS*

As its name suggests, this is a small species which does not exceed 2 m ($6\frac{1}{2}$ ft) in length. Found in parts of Central and Western Africa, the dwarf crocodile remains a rather mysterious species, which has not been well studied. It is clear, however, that these small crocodiles prefer swampland and slow-flowing stretches of water, rather than open rivers, in contrast to the African slender-snouted crocodile. They tend to show established homing instincts and, although they may occasionally venture away from their immediate environment, they will generally return to the same locality. Dwarf crocodiles are most likely to be seen on land after dark, and generally avoid basking for long periods. Occasionally, they may climb trees to sun themselves. If threatened, the crocodiles will retreat to holes in a nearby bank, which they may have dug previously.

Fig. 22   Distribution of the dwarf crocodile (*Osteolaemus tetraspis*).

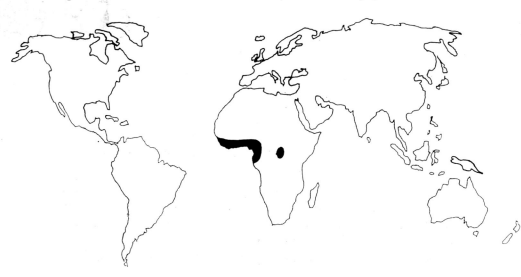

Plate 72   The smallest of the crocodiles, the dwarf species (*Osteolaemus tetraspis*), has been little studied, and much still remains to be learned about its lifestyle. It seems to be more terrestrial than many species and probably hunts on land.

The feeding preferences of the dwarf crocodile are unclear, although it does take fish and amphibians, and may catch prey on land. Rarely are numbers of these crocodiles found together, although pairs come together prior to the nesting period, which appears to be concentrated in May and June, at least on the Ivory Coast. The female builds a mound which measures approximately 1.5 m (5 ft) in diameter. The number of eggs laid is relatively small, ranging from about 10 up to 17 and each measuring 7 cm ($2\frac{3}{4}$ in) long.

Their patterns of guarding and hatching do not appear to differ

177

significantly from those of other crocodiles, although females prove more defensive than the African slender-snouted crocodile. The hatchlings will emerge from 12 weeks onwards, measuring about 28 cm (11 in) by this stage. It is thought that their mother then protects them when they enter the water.

For a period of time, a separate species, christened *Osteoblepharon osborni*, was recognized, from the north-east of Zaïre, but this is now usually grouped with *Osteolaemus tetraspis*, although some taxonomists accord it subspecific status. There are some significant differences, in terms of the patterning of scales on the neck for example, and the structure of the nasal region between these two populations.

In view of its small size, and the presence of ventral osteoderms, the dwarf crocodile has never been extensively hunted for its skin. But there is now some evidence to suggest that the level of trade may be increasing, as the numbers of Nile crocodiles have fallen. It is a relatively docile crocodilian and may be caught without too much difficulty. Some individuals are stuffed on their demise to become tasteless tourist souvenirs, while others are killed for food. There is no reliable population estimate for this species, although in some countries, such as the Central African Republic, a decline in numbers during recent years is apparent.

FALSE GHARIAL   *TOMISTOMA SCHLEGELII*
The last of an ancient line of crocodiles, dating back to the Eocene

Fig. 23   Distribution of the false gharial (*Tomistoma schlegelii*).

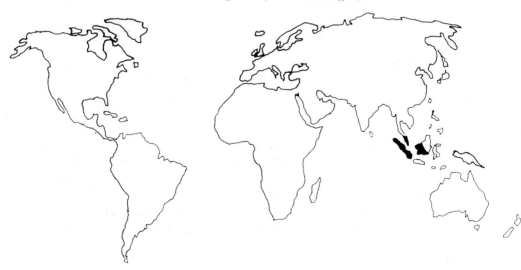

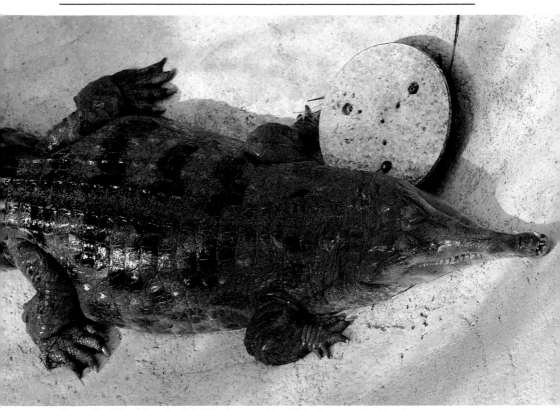

Plate 73   The false gharial (*Tomistoma schlegelii*) is characterized by its very narrow snout. It is a rare species in the wild.

epoch, about 57 million years ago, this species is believed to range from the southern part of Thailand across the Malay Peninsula to Borneo and Sumatra, although it may already be extinct in Thailand. It was probably distributed over a wider area in the past, extending as far north as Guangdong (Kwangtung) in China, where remains of this species, dating back to the Ming dynasty, which ended in 1644, have been discovered.

The false gharial is a freshwater crocodile, resembling the gharial with its slender snout. It is relatively dark in coloration, with black markings both on the body and the snout, and can grow to 4 m (13 ft) in length. One individual measuring nearly 1.8 m (6 ft) was caught in Malaysia at the end of the 1970s, but here, as elsewhere throughout its range, the false gharial is now rarely encountered. The diet of this species is comprised mainly of fish, although other small vertebrates may also be taken.

When breeding, females construct a nest of dry leaves, which may be up to 60 cm (24 in) in height. The nest site is usually quite close to water, but often in a shaded spot. Between 20 and 60 eggs form a typical clutch, with incubation lasting for about three months. The hatchlings receive no parental help and, perhaps not surprisingly, many die at this early stage. Nests are often raided by various lizards and wild pigs, even before the young crocodiles have emerged.

The skin trade may have played a part in the decline of the false gharial, but environmental factors have also clearly been significant. Habitat loss because of direct human encroachment and an increase in rice cultivation has been a major problem. In Indonesia, over-collection of juveniles for rearing purposes may also have been significant.

Much still remains to be learnt about this species. A valuable group are housed and are breeding at the Samutprakan Crocodile Farm in Thailand, and the false gharial is also represented in various zoological collections. A reasonable population may even survive in Sumatra, where it was found to be locally common in the east of the country, following a survey carried out in 1981.

Chapter 9

The Gharial

GHARIAL *GAVIALIS GANGETICUS*

The gharials, also known as garials or gavials – of the sub-family Gavialiae – are represented today by only one species. The long, slender snout of this species has interlocking teeth and, in this instance, adult males can be recognized by the presence of a noticeable swelling at the top of their upper jaw. The gharial is primarily aquatic, as shown by the pronounced webbing between its toes, and the lack of musculature in its legs.

Its centre of distribution has been in the northern part of the Indian sub-continent, notably within the major river drainages here, which include the Ganges, Irrawady, Brahmaputra and Bhima, within the borders of India, Pakistan, Bangladesh and Nepal. The gharial is now extinct in Bhutan, however, with its last remaining strongholds being the Rapti-Narayani River in Nepal and several Indian rivers, notably the Girwa, Chambal and Ganges.

These are potentially very slender, long crocodilians, capable of growing to lengths of 6.5 m (21 ft). One shot in January 1924, in the Kosi River in north Bihar, measured 7.1 m (23 ft 7 in), and gigantic gharials of 9.1 m (30 ft) have been claimed in the past, but without reliable evidence. Nevertheless it is clear from their fossilized remains

Fig. 24   Distribution of the gharial (*Gavialis gangeticus*).

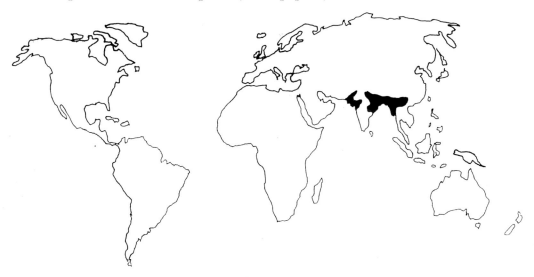

181

that today's gharials are relatively small as some in the past have exceeded 17 m (56 ft) long. They are not aggressive crocodilians, however, and feed predominantly on fish. These are clamped by the sharp teeth in its narrow mouth, while the gharial raises its head above water and deftly repositions its prey so that it can be swallowed head first. Birds are also sometimes taken, notably by older gharials.

During the early part of the century, hunting contributed to the gharial's decline. It had been fashionable for Indian royalty to hunt these crocodilians for many years, but then systematic slaughter for their skins followed. More recently, the fast-flowing rivers which the gharial inhabits have been dammed, both for irrigation and hydro-electric power purposes. Since it could no longer nest in the adjoining banks, the gharial population inevitably declined still further.

The effects of such development are clearly demonstrated by the case of the Ramganga River, which used to support a large number of gharials. The building of a dam at Kalagarh, which was finally completed in 1974, meant that little water flowed beyond this site and areas of gharial habitat upstream were also lost, because of the flooding over a wide area. Damage to the banks, caused by blasting during the construction phase resulted in irreversible loss of nesting habitat. No gharials are now thought to be breeding here and just a few individuals remain.

Inhabiting areas which have seen large population increases, gharials also face direct and indirect human predation. Their eggs are still sought after as a source of food, and are also considered to have valuable medicinal properties. Similarly, male gharials tend to be hunted, because their snouts are said to have aphrodisiac properties. Gharials also become enmeshed in fishing nets, and drown, or may be killed by the fishermen when the nets are hauled in. But the decline in the gharial population has had a detrimental effect on their catches. This is because the gharials fed mainly on predatory fish and, in their absence, the numbers of these have risen, reducing the numbers of edible fish in the rivers.

Serious efforts are now being made, however, to ensure the survival of the gharial, with some noticeable success. By 1974, the total population of these crocodilians, both in the wild and captivity, was less than 250 individuals. Since then, it has risen in excess of 2500, although a risk remains because there are probably fewer than 20 adult males at present.

This scheme has relied upon the artificial hatching and rearing of gharials, which are then released back into the wild. Their main area of secure habitat in India is in the National Chambal Sanctuary, where over 900 juveniles have been released. The river system here extends to over 600 km (372 miles) in length, offering adequate refuge for a reasonable population. Elsewhere, in Nepal, a colony of 20 adults is protected within the confines of the Chitwan National Park, where they inhabit the Rapti-Narayani River.

Captive breeding has been achieved on several occasions now, and the gharial in time may be farmed, bearing in mind the lack of available protected habitat within its former range. Its name, 'gharial', originates from a native word *ghara*, which describes the handle on a pot, popular in the north of India. It refers in this instance to the swelling present at the tip of the male's snout.

Plate 74   Captive breeding of endangered crocodilians offers hope for their survival in the short term, with the ultimate aim being to repopulate safe areas where previously they may have been hunted to extinction. The gharial is one species which has already benefited from a management programme of this type.

Further Reading

Although a number of the titles in this list are out of print, they should be available from a specialist natural history book dealer, or possibly from your local library.

Behler, J. L. & King, F. W. (1979) *The Audubon Society Field Guide to North American Reptiles and Amphibians* Alfred A. Knopf, New York.

Bellairs, A. d'A. (1969) *The Life of Reptiles* Volumes 1 & 2 Weidenfeld & Nicolson, London.

Bellairs, A. d'A. & Cox, C. B. (Eds) (1976) *Morphology and Biology of Reptiles* Academic Press, London.

Branch, B. (1988) *Field Guide to the Snakes and Other Reptiles of Southern Africa* New Holland, London.

Cogger, H. G. (1983) *Reptiles and Amphibians of Australia* A. H. & A. W. Reed, Sydney.

Conant, R. (1975) *A Field Guide to Reptiles and Amphibians of Eastern and Central America* Houghton Mifflin & Co., Boston.

Cooper, J. E. & Jackson, O. F. (1981) *Diseases of Reptilia* Volumes 1 & 2 Academic Press, London.

Cox, B. (Ed.) (1988) *Macmillan Illustrated Encyclopedia of Dinosaurs and Prehistoric Animals* Macmillan, London.

Daniel, J. C. (1983) *The Book of Indian Reptiles* Bombay Natural History Society, Bombay.

Ditmars, R. L. (1953) *The Reptiles of North America* Doubleday, New York.

Earl, L. (1954) *Crocodile Fever* Alfred A. Knopf, New York.

Edwards, H. (1988) *Crocodile Attack in Australia* Swan Publishing, Sydney.

Eri, V. (1973) *The Crocodile* Penguin, Ringwood, Australia.

Frazier, S. & Cox, J. (1989) *The FAO-PHPA Crocodile Management Project: Development of the Crocodile Skin Industry on a Sustainable Basis in Indonesia* FAO & PHPA, Indonesia.

Frankfort, H. (1961) *Ancient Egyptian Religion* Harper Torchbooks, New York.

Fuchs, K. H. (1974) *The Chemistry and Technology of Novelty Leathers* FAO, Rome.

Gans, C. L. (Ed.) (1969–82) *Biology of the Reptilia* Volumes 1–13 Academic Press, London.

Goin, C. J. & O. B. & Zug, G.R. (1978) *Introduction to Herpetology* W. H. Freeman, San Francisco.

Graham, A. & Beard, P. (1973) *Eyelids of the Morning: The Mingled Destinies of Crocodiles and Men* A. & W. Visual Library, New York.

Groombridge, B. (Ed.) (1982) *The IUCN Red Data Book: Part I Testudines, Crocodylia, Rhynocephalia* IUCN, Gland Switzerland.

Guggisberg, C. A. W. (1972) *Crocodiles: Their Natural History, Folklore and Conservation* David & Charles, Newton Abbot, England.

Halliday, T. & Adler, K. (Eds) (1986) *The Encyclopaedia of Reptiles and Amphibians* George Allen & Unwin, London.

International Union for the Conservation of Nature and Natural Resources (1971) *Crocodiles: Proceedings of the First Working Meeting of Crocodile Specialists* Volume I and subsequent publications in this series. IUCN, Gland, Switzerland.

International Union for the Conservation of Nature and Natural Resources (1985) *Identification Manual of the Convention on International Trade in Endangered Species of Wild Fauna and Flora* IUCN, Gland, Switzerland.

International Union for the Conservation of Nature and Natural Resources (1989) *Crocodiles: Their Ecology, Management and Conservation* IUCN, Gland, Switzerland.

Katz, S. & P. (1977) *Alligator* Sphere Books, London.

Lewinsohn, R. (1954) *Animals, Men and Myths* Victor Gollancz, London.

Luxmoore, R. A., Barzdo, J. G., Broad, S. R. & Jones, D. A. (1985) *A Directory of Crocodilian Farming Operations* IUCN Wildlife Trade Monitoring Unit, Cambridge, England.

Luxmoore, R. A., Groombridge, B. & Broad, S. R. (Eds) (1988) *Significant Trade in Wildlife: A Review of Selected Species Listed in CITES Appendix II.* Volume 2: Reptiles and Invertebrates IUCN/CITES, Lausanne, Switzerland.

McIlhenney, E. A. (1935) *The Alligator's Life History* Christopher Publishing House, Boston.

Mertens, R. (1960) *The World of Amphibians and Reptiles* McGraw-Hill, New York.

Meter, V. B. V. (1987) *Florida's Alligators and Crocodiles* Florida Power and Light Company, Miami.

Minton, S. A. jun. & M. R. (1973) *Giant Reptiles* Charles Scribner's Sons, New York.

Murphy, J. B. & Collins, J. T. (Eds) (1980) *Reproductive Biology and Diseases of Captive Reptiles* Society for the Study of Reptiles and Amphibians (SSAR), Ohio.

National Research Council (1983) *Managing Tropical Animal Resources: Crocodiles as a Resource for the Tropics* National Academy Press, Washington, D.C.

Neill, W. T. (1971) *The Last of the Ruling Reptiles* Columbia University Press, New York.

Nicol, J. (1984) *The Ganges Gharial* Channel Four Television, London.

Pooley, A. C. (1982) *The Biology of the Nile Crocodile* (Crocodylus niloticus) *in Zululand* M.Sc. dissertation for the University of Natal, Pietermaritzburg.

Pooley, A. C. (1982) *Discoveries of a Crocodile Man* Collins, Johannesburg.

Pope, C. H. (1964) *The Reptile World* Alfred A. Knopf, New York.

Ross, C. A. (Ed.) (1989) *Crocodiles and Alligators* Merehurst Press, London.

Schmidt, K. P & Inger, R. F. (1957) *Living Reptiles of the World* Hamish Hamilton, London.

Steel, R. (1989) *Crocodiles* Christopher Helm Publishers, Bromley, London.

Webb, G. J. W., Manolis, S. C. & Whitehead, P. J. (Eds) (1987) *Wildlife Management: Crocodiles and Alligators* Surrey Beatty, Sydney.

Webb, G. J. W. & Manolis, S. C. (1989) *Crocodiles of Australia* Reed Books, Frenchs Forest, Australia.

Willis, R. (1974) *Man and Beast* Basic Books, New York.

Wood, G. L. (1982) *The Guinness Book of Animal Facts and Feats* Guinness Superlatives, Enfield, London.

Index

Numbers in *italic* refer to black and white illustrations.
Numbers in **bold** refer to colour plates.